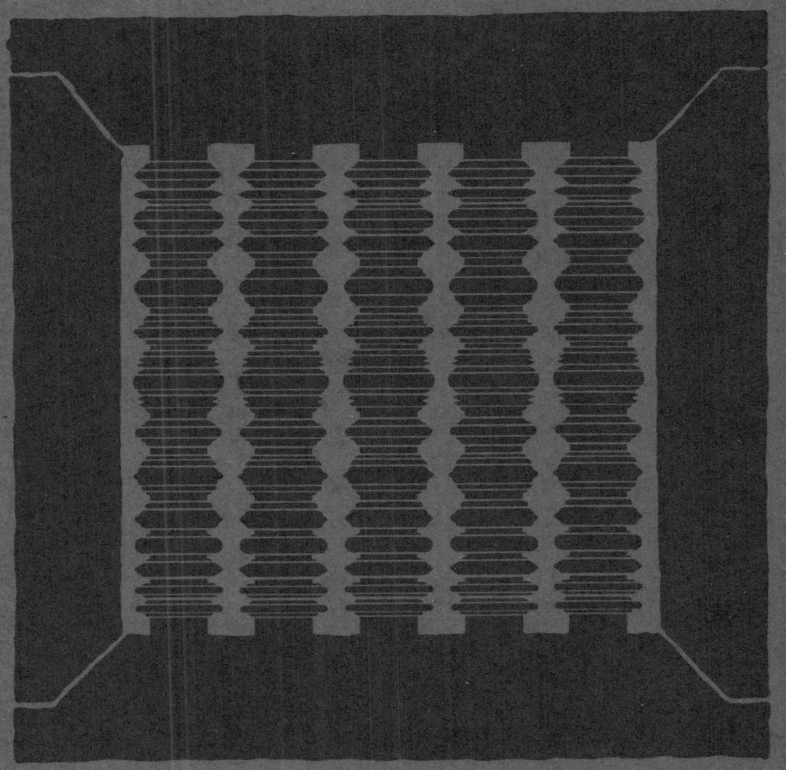

PALACES OF·THE·GODS

KHMER ART & ARCHITECTURE IN THAILAND

PALACES
OF · THE · GODS

KHMER ART & ARCHITECTURE IN THAILAND

SMITTHI SIRIBHADRA · ELIZABETH MOORE
PHOTOGRAPHY MICHAEL FREEMAN
RIVER BOOKS · BANGKOK

Front Cover
The central sanctuary and western gallery, Phimai, 11th century.

Back Cover
Gopura V at Preah Vihear, 10th century.

Previous Page *East entrance gopura at Phnom Rung with 'naga bridge' in foreground, 12th century.*

First edition published and distributed in Thailand

by Asia Books Co., Ltd
5 Sukhumvit Road Soi 61
Bangkok 10110, Thailand
PO Box 40
Tel 391 2680 Fax 381 1621

A River Books Production

Designed by Richard Ward
Photography by Michael Freeman

Editor Narisa Chakra
Production supervision Paisarn Piemmettawat

Typesetting by Noël Teale / Mac & Co UK

Printed and bound in Thailand by Amarin Printing Group.

ISBN 974 8303 19 5

CONTENTS

Buddha sheltered by Naga, sandstone, 13th century. Prasat Phimai.

FOREWORD

Khmer temples in Thailand are evidently a challenging field to explore, yet no attempt has been made to study them systematically. Thus, the appearance of *Palaces of the Gods: Khmer Art & Architecture in Thailand* is indeed an occasion to celebrate.

The authors, by using two crucial disciplines: Art History and Architecture, have successfully presented an authoritative work on the subject. Even though they have been obliged to employ the dating system established using archaeological data found in Cambodia to study Khmer art in Thailand, careful observations and comments are exhaustively provided to remind the readers of the differences. They have also made provoking and interesting suggestions on the classification of Khmer art especially concerning the Khleang and Baphuon styles.

I hope that this book will be very useful to the study of Khmer art and increase interest in Khmer studies in Thailand.

Sirindhorn

HRH Princess Maha Chakri Sirindhorn
September 1992

CHINA
Hong Kong
BURMA
Hanoi
Hai Phong
LAOS
Gulf of Tonkin
Chiang Mai
Vientiane
Rangoon
THAILAND
Khon Kaen
Da Nang
Nakhon Ratchasima
VIETNAM
Bangkok
ANDAMAN SEA
KAMPUCHEA
Phnom Penh
Gulf of Thailand
Saigon
SOUTH CHINA SEA
Straits of Malacca
MALAYSIA
BRUNEI
Medan
Kuala Lumpur
SARAWAK
Singapore
SUMATRA
Pontianak
BORNEO
Banjarmasin
Palembang
INDIAN OCEAN
JAVA SEA
Jakarta
JAVA

INTRODUCTION

The stone temples of the Khmer were palaces for the gods. The gods were not drawn to the temple in search of earthly chambers to inhabit or long halls to walk. Nor did the Khmer temple offer vast audience halls for congregation. The aim of the Khmer temple was far more ambitious - to recreate the universe of the gods. The temple complex was the visualisation of a doctrine which united king and god, a material demonstration of harmony in this world and the next.

A transformation of ritual activity occurred in Khmer society in the late 1st millenium AD. This change centred around the temple : not only the pivot of religious rites, but, in the guise of a mountain, the pivot of the universe. To the Khmer, ritual was inseparable from belief. The construction of the temple did not demonstrate the religious fervour of the people, but created belief in the act of ritual.

To appreciate the ruins of the Khmer temples which remain today, the contemporary history and religion of the Khmer require introduction. However, first a word about the need for this book. The Khmer peoples today are primarily found in the country of Cambodia (formerly Kambuja) but the original heartland of the Khmer was associated with an area of the middle Mekong river in Laos and the southern part of Northeast Thailand. Thus while the remains of Khmer temples at Angkor are justly famous and rulers from at least the 9th to 14th centuries concentrated their temples within the urban area of Angkor, throughout this period, if not far before, the Khmer also inhabited parts of Thailand, Laos and Cambodia.

Use of the Khmer language in early Southeast Asia probably extended far beyond the limits of present-day Cambodia, into the Mekong delta, the Khorat Plateau of Northeast Thailand, and central Thailand's lower Chao Phraya valley. It is possible that a proto-Khmer language was spoken by the peoples of Funan, a 1st to 5th century AD kingdom located in the lower Mekong of southern Cambodia. How these peoples reached the area is unclear, but similarities in the material cultures of Northeast Thailand and Cambodia by the beginning of the Christian era suggest a shared heritage originating at a much earlier date.

During the early first millennium AD, the adoption of aspects of Indian civilization had a profound affect on the nature of Khmer urban settlement. Indian imports included concepts of kingship and law, the use of Sanskrit in the recording of inscriptions on stone, and most especially, the Hindu and Buddhist religions with their

Opposite
This famous statue of King Jayavarman VII (AD 1181-c.1219), the last great ruler and builder of the Khmer empire, was found at Phimai and underlines the links which existed between this city in Thailand's Northeast and Cambodia. Jayavarman VII was from the Mahidharapura dynasty of Northeast Thailand.

distinctive styles of art and architecture. For example, the word for 'brick' in Thailand developed from the Sanskrit, and the erection of brick and stone structures to honor deities may date to the advent of Indian religious influence. Previously shrines were made of wood, a custom which still survives in rural areas of Thailand where small wooden shelters house the spirits of the land. The building of these shrines would be undertaken by the whole community and like Hindu and Buddhist temples were part of a ritual complex designed to ensure the continued prosperity of the society.

The construction of Khmer temples in Thailand represented not only the founding of a religious shrine, but the incorporation of a community to serve the gods and rulers to whom the centre was dedicated. The building of stone temples with small inner cells to house a cult image is clearly modelled on Indian prototypes. However, the tradition of ancestor veneration is deeply ingrained in the culture of the Khmer peoples. Thus the temples of the Khmer represented an amalgamation of established customs of ancestor and spirit veneration with imported ideas which continued from the 8th to the 12th centuries. At the end of the 12th century, Jayavarman VII erected two massive temples honouring his parents: Ta Prohm was dedicated to his mother in 1186 AD and five years later, Preah Khan was dedicated to his father.

The high esteem accorded at royal courts to religious figures was crucial in the blending of Hinduism and Buddhism with pre-existing ancestor cults. The many Indian concepts of state and kingship adopted by the Khmer also reflect the political power of priests. A mutually beneficial liason existed between the king and his religious advisors, the first of whom may have reached the Khmer courts in the early 1st millenium AD. Some scholars argue that the earliest Indian advisors to Southeast Asia were Buddhist missionaries who arrived in the wake of Indian traders. As one of the characteristics of the absorbtion of Indian religions in Southeast Asia has been toleration, Buddhism, Hinduism, and earlier beliefs appear to have co-existed peaceably, a rare state of affairs in the face of priestly activity limited to religious conversion. This implies that religious advisors and rulers were equally concerned with earthly and immortal existence, a concept whose essence is expressed in the term 'devaraja', a Sanskrit word meaning 'god who is king'. A Khmer ruler would be consecrated as a devaraja by the court priest and would take a Sanskrit-based name, such as Jaya- (victorious) or Surya- (from the sun god Surya). To this he would add the suffix -varman, meaning 'protector'. The ruler would commemorate the event with inscriptions, and the foundation of a temple. For the most part, the temples of the Khmer rulers were dedicated to Hindu gods, principally Shiva and Vishnu. However this did not exclude incorporation of other religious elements, and traces of a variety of Buddhist doctrines may be seen in many Khmer temples. In the late 12th century, Jayavarman VII (1181-1219) adopted Mahayana Buddhism as his state religion. Thus during this period, architecture and scupture show their greatest development in Buddhist rather than Hindu iconography.

1 THE KHMER CIVILISATION

RELIGION

Principal Deities of the Hindu and Buddhist Religions

Opposite
Shiva, who plays a central role in Hindu cosmology and Khmer iconography is here shown dancing in a scene from the eastern pediment of Phnom Rung. The rhythms of Shiva's dancing were believed to represent the continual birth, death and rebirth of the universe.

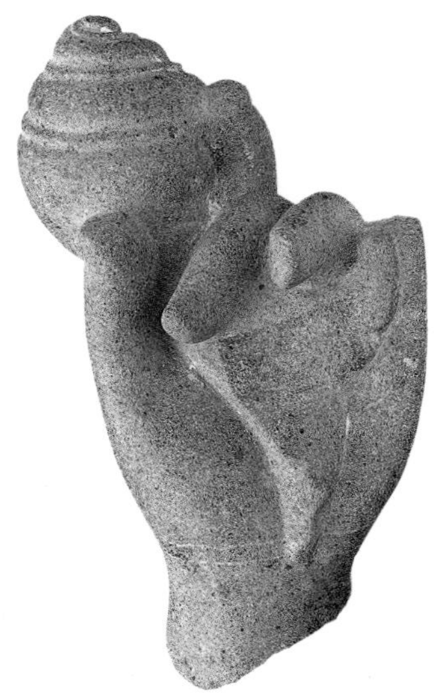

Hand of Vishnu holding conch shell, stone. (Mahavirawong Museum, Khorat)

The Hindu religion of modern India has its roots in the pre-Aryan animism of that country. The development over time of complex rituals led to the establishment of a powerful caste of Brahman priests, and the formulation of an intricate philosophical system. At a simple level, much of this centres on cycles of birth and rebirth, and is personified in the three major Hindu deities, Brahma, Vishnu and Shiva, with their ability to present themselves in various incarnations.

Brahma, Vishnu and Shiva

Brahma is the Creator, endowed with four faces, allowing him to survey the four quarters of the world. He carries objects in his many hands, these attributes and his multiple limbs symbolising his divinity. The attributes sometimes vary, but generally include a water jug. Brahma's mount is the sacred goose or hamsa, whose flight is said to join the watery world with the heavens above.

Vishnu, the Preserver, has as his mount the mythical Garuda bird. The Garuda is arch-enemy of the naga who rule the subterranean world. This is another example, as is the temple, of the continual ideal of uniting upper and lower realms of the universe. Vishnu's attributes include the discus and the conch. While Brahma and Shiva are generally depicted upright, Vishnu is often seen in a reclining position on Khmer lintels. He is accompanied by his consort, Lakshmi or Sri, who is said to have been born during the 'Churning of the Sea of Milk' (see below), part of the cycle of creation and destruction, when Vishnu is incarnated as a tortoise.

One of the most popular of the ten incarnations of Vishnu in Khmer imagery is that of Rama, the principal character of the ancient Indian epic, the Ramayana. This tells the story of Rama, including his birth, the abduction of his wife Sita by the demon Ravana, and her eventual recapturing by Rama, with the invaluable aid of the monkeys, led by Hanuman the white monkey king.

The third major deity of the Hindu triumvirate is Shiva, god of the destruction which must precede creation. Shiva's vital energy is depicted as a stylised phallus, or linga. This is often divided into three parts, each representing one of the gods: the square base is Brahma, an octagonal prism Vishnu, and the rounded cylinder and point being Shiva. The linga was often originally mounted erect on a pedestal symbolising the yoni, or female organ. A conduit known as a somasutra facilitated drainage of ritual waters poured over the linga.

Shiva is also depicted anthropomorphically, most easily identified by his third eye. He often carries a trident or axe, wears a snake across his chest, and may have matted hair. Sometimes both Shiva and Vishnu are combined in the same statue, known as Hari-hara. Shiva's mount is the bull Nandin, and his consort is Parvati. Their sons are the elephant-headed Ganesha, god of knowledge and Kartikeya, god of war.

Buddhism

The Buddhist religion originated with the person of Prince Siddartha Gautama of the Sakya clan in the 6th century BC at Lumbhini in present day Nepal. Born into a life of great luxury and shielded from all suffering, as a grown man, Prince Siddartha abandoned his royal life to become a wandering ascetic. He finally achieved enlightenment to become a Buddha ('the enlightened one') through meditation, which revealed to him that the cause of all suffering was desire. The Buddha taught his doctrine for almost 50 years, gathering a large following of disciples and dying at the age of eighty.

After his death, the doctrine was at first passed on orally. When the texts were written down, two canons emerged, one in Pali and the other in Sanskrit. Two schools of Buddhism also developed, the Theravada and the Mahayana. The person of the Buddha as an historical figure is central to the Theravada canon, the doctrine which forms the present religions of Thailand, Burma and Sri Lanka. In the Mahayana canon, the religion adopted by the Khmer especially under Jayavarman VII (AD 1181-1219), the emphasis on the individuality of the historical Buddha is less, and he is one of a number of Bodhisattvas, or Buddhas-to-be, who achieved enlightment. Female divinites such as Prajñaparamita, goddess of perfect wisdom, also play a vital role in Mahayana Buddhism.

In Khmer sculpture one of the most popular motifs from the life of the Buddha Sakyamuni is that of Buddha being sheltered by the naga or serpent Muchalinda.

Naga

Stories involving the naga or serpent are found in both Hindu and Buddhist mythology. Their popularity in Khmer art is striking. The underwater kingdoms of the naga are formed by the rivers, lakes and seas of the world, and here these kingly beings inhabit luxurious palaces studded with pearls and gems. The naga is not only keeper of the life energy stored in the waters, but also guardian of corals, shells and pearls, and carries one jewel in his head.

The sinuous form of the naga creates arches around pediments, the balustrades around ponds and flanking causeways. Such causeways are often referred to as 'naga bridges', but in all these instances, the elongated tube of the naga's body symbolises the

11th century gable fragment showing Umamahesvara - Shiva and his consort Uma, riding on the bull Nandin. (Phimai Museum)

11th century gable fragment showing Indra riding the three-headed elephant Airavata. (Phimai Museum)

rainbow linking the human and divine worlds. The significance of the naga derives from the puranas or ancient stories of India. However, the popularity of the beast in Khmer art stems from the pre-Indian belief in the spirits of the land and water. With the dissemination of Indian religions into Khmer lands about two thousand years ago, Indian iconography offered a variety of ways to express these spirits, as well as incorporating local dynastic histories, and Hindu and Buddhist stories.

The legendary geneaology of many of the Khmer rulers has been preserved in Sanskrit eulogies inscribed on large stone slabs. Many proclaim their right to the throne by citing descent from the union of an Indian brahmin, or wise man, with a nagini, half-serpent half-woman daughter of the naga king. Having planted his spear to take control of the land, his mastery of the waters is established through the naga.

In Hindu mythology, the world cycle is composed of four kalpa, or ages. After creation, fourteen intervals relentlessly move towards destruction. During the sixth interval of the present age, the gods and demons were battling for world dominion, when a truce was called in order to extract amrita, the elixir of immortality from the cosmic ocean. This episode was referred to as the Churning of the Sea of Milk and in it Mount Mandara is used as a pivot to stir the sea of Milk. The body of the naga Vasuki is wrapped around Mount Mandara and with gods and demons pulling at either end, the serpent causes the mountain to turn and the elixir to be drawn forth from the ocean.

At the end of the age, destruction begins. The energy of Vishnu first becomes the sun, drying earth of all life. He then is the wind, sucking up all the air, igniting fire, and turning all to ash. As a great cloud, Vishnu then sheds rain, the sweet milk of the cosmic ocean. Here the ashes of creation are stored, and all is dissolved, including the moon and stars, into an endless sheet of water. The age is now night, as long as has been the day. In his human form, Vishnu sleeps upon the naga, the five-headed Ananta ('Endless') or Sesha ('Remainder') symbolizing the cosmic fluid of creation.

Within the water is slowly gathered the five elements of energy: ether, air, fire, water and earth. Vishnu stirs, and the rippling waters form a cleft. Wind rushes into the space, creates a friction with the waters, and produces a fire which devours the water. A heavenly space is created in the void where Vishnu rests. A lotus springs from his navel, upon which is seated the god-creator Brahma, his four faces controlling all sides of the universe. The world cycle then begins anew.

As mentioned earlier, the naga's arch enemy is the Garuda and the two are frequently depicted together as rivals, the naga clasped in the Garuda's claws.

The naga also appears in the story of the life of the historical Buddha. During the meditation of the Lord Buddha, a violent storm arose. The seven-headed serpent king, Muchalinda, issued forth from the roots of the tree where the Buddha was seated and wound his coils seven times in protection, raising his heads to form a protective hood until the floods subsided. The Buddha thus elicited devotion from the naga, and the life-giving waters which he ruled. Khmer depictions of the Buddha seated on the naga became a common motif as early as the 11th and particularly in the late 12th

Early 12th century lintel from Phimai showing a scene from the Ramayana - Nagapasa, in which Rama and Lakshamana are entrapped by the coils of the naga's body.

Shiva linga on pedestal 12th-14th century. (Prasat Phu Prasat, Ubon)

Stone Ganesha, early 10th century. (Non Kalen, Ubon)

century, with the adoption of Buddhism by the last of the great kings of Angkor, Jayavarman VII. The image of the Buddha being sheltered by the serpent was particularly popular in Northeast Thailand and may stem from the very ancient local culture of the area.

Kala

Another creature seen throughout the chronology of Khmer art is the kala. Many interpretations have been given to the face of the kala which so often forms the centerpiece of Khmer lintels and pediments.The creature is also referred to as kirtimukha, from two Sanskrit words, kirti, meaning 'glory' and mukha meaning 'face'. He can be seen protecting temple doorways from India, to Thailand, Cambodia and Indonesia, where he is sometimes referred to as Panaspati. In all cases, his rounded face has a wide jaw, prominent teeth, and large flared nostrils in a lion-like nose. Sometimes a lower jaw is present, but often only his large triangular tongue can be seen extended to support the weight of the garland issuing from his mouth.

Indian legends relate that the voracious kala demanded a victim of Shiva. The god was enraged by the request and ordered the creature to devour himself. The gluttonous kala proceeded to consume himself, until only his body and hands were left. Shiva then ordered him to serve as guardian of temple entries as a reminder of the god's power to protect or destroy. In this interpretation, the kala causes one to consider whether one's own life and deeds are worthy of the gods.

Many kalas such as those at Muang Tam also have hands and arms, even bracelets upon occasion, to hold the garland firmly in place. It is this aspect of the creature which adds confusion to the iconography, for the presence of arms and hands is often associated with the demon Rahu. While the origins of the kirtimukha or kala are often linked to Shiva, the Hindu god of creation and destruction, the legend of Rahu involves Vishnu, the protector. Rahu is said to have stolen some amrita from the gods. He drank some of the precious liquid from the cup but was seen and recognised by the sun and the moon. The angry Vishnu then killed Rahu, cutting off his head. However, because the amrita had already touched his lips, Rahu's head had become immortal. Disembodied, Rahu became a planet and forever tries to take revenge on the sun and moon by attempting to eat them. Upon occasion he succeeds, swallows them whole, and causes an eclipse. Without a body to enter, the sun or the moon soon reappear, ending the eclipse, and forcing Rahu to take up his quest once more.

So is it the face of the kirtimukha or that of Rahu that protects the Khmer temple? Thai art historians have various opinions. Some call it the kirtimukha or the 'lion face' (simhamukha) with arms and hands, palms raised up and facing outwards. The protruding eyes are seen as reminiscent of yakshas, sometimes benevolent, sometimes fearsome guardian spirits. Others associate it with the story of Rahu, despite the absence of a sun or moon in the creature's mouth. It may be that aspects of various mythical

Bronze head of Buddha 13th century. (Khonkaen Museum)

Bronze Vishnu on garuda, 12th century, (Khonkaen Museum)

Bronze Buddha in meditation 13th century. (National Museum, Bangkok)

Bronze Ganesha, 12th century. (Khonkaen Museum)

Lokesvara,
mid-12th century.
(National Museum, Bangkok)

Above *Brahma, Baphuon style, 11th century. (National Museum, Bangkok)*

Opposite *Bronze Buddha, 13th century. (National Museum, Bangkok)*

Stone naga from the pediment end of the central tower at Sikhoraphum, 12th century.

Below
Kala from the lintel over the entrance to the central courtyard, Phimai, early 12th century.

beings contributed to the Khmer version, welcoming pilgrims praising the gods, and demonically deflecting evil from the sacred precinct.

In Indonesia, and in some of the earliest Khmer lintels, the kala is often flanked by a pair of makara, a composite animal with the body of a crocodile and snout of an elephant. The makara, like the kala, spews foliage, and is generally considered aquatic from his reptilian origins.

Opposite
The Louvo (Lopburi) contingent in the parade of the Khmer army. These were the regional troops garrisonned in Lopburi in the central Chao Phraya valley. From the south wall of the gallery, Angkor Wat, 12th century.

THE KHMER CIVILISATION

HISTORY
The Khmer in Thailand: 6th to 9th Century

The earliest inscriptions of Khmer history in Northeast Thailand date to the end of the 6th century AD. One found in the province of Surin, north of Ta Muen, was erected by a king called Mahendravarman. The inscription, written in Sanskrit, commemorates the installation of an image of Shiva's bull Nandin. Mahendravarman ordered the inscription carved after he had conquered 'all the country'. Scholars are still debating about what territory was vanquished by Mahendravarman, with many attempts being made to assign a specific location to cities mentioned in other inscriptions found within Cambodia.

The other source of information on this period are Chinese accounts, and references in these to tributary states such as Funan and Chenla have been subject to similar attempts to place them geographically. Traditionally, Funan is dated to the 1st to 5th century AD, and is said to have included southern parts of present day South Vietnam and Cambodia. Chenla, from about the 6th to 8th century, is placed more to the north: northern Cambodia, middle Laos and the southern part of Northeast Thailand. More recently, epigraphical analysis has shown that Funan and Chenla were only one of a number of polities, and that the domain controlled by rulers of these societies were in constant flux depending on the fortunes of the moment.

The inscriptions erected by Mahendravarman provide an example of this process, for after what appears to have been a flurry of campaigns and proclamations of success, a hiatus of several hundred years occurs. What is more, no temples in Thailand which are known at present can be dated to the end of the 6th century. The earliest structures, such as Prasat Phumphon in Surin province date to the 7th century, but are not associated with any inscriptions.

No Khmer temples in Thailand can be dated to the intervening 8th and 9th centuries. Nonetheless, numerous polities of Mon and Khmer peoples existed on the Khorat Plateau and in fact, a clear-cut distinction between the two groups prior to about 1000 AD does not appear to be justified. Evidence of this proto-Mon/Khmer culture includes a few inscriptions, remains of irregular cities enclosed by moats and earthen ramparts, Buddha images, and large boundary stones carved with Buddhist scenes. Both the Buddhist culture to the north of the Dangrek mountains and the Hindu cults which prospered to the south represented the absorption of far more than a religious system. Indian scripts such as Pali and Sanskrit were used for sacred inscriptions. Mon and

Below
Stone stele (sanskrit) from the Ku Noi hospital, Khonkaen museum, 13th century. The stele was discovered in the excavations at Ku Noi and states that this site was a hospital in the time of Jayvarman VII. The bottom part of the stele is broken and missing. There are three different sizes of hospital steles - large, medium and small. Ku Noi is in the middle group. All the steles gave details regarding the hospital, such as the number of doctors, nurses, and types of offerings, etc.

Khmer scripts developed from these and offered a means of writing the spoken language of the time. In addition, other aspects of Indian culture were absorbed such as literature, mathematics, astronomy and astrology. Although evidence of much of this material culture has disappeared, the result of the stimulus provided by Indian art and architecture remains in the temples of the Khmer.

The Bakong is the earliest surviving state temple built by Indravarman I for the Devaraja cult. It is situated close to Angkor by the shores of the Great Lake, 9th century.

Jayavarman II and the Devaraja cult

In contrast with the paucity of Khmer temple remains in Thailand prior to about the 10th century, a succession of temple sites in Cambodia are linked to the political consolidation of the Khmer. One important site was the 7th century capital of Isanavarman I at Sambor Prei Kuk, to the east of the Tonlé Sap Great Lake. However, the founding of the Khmer capital is traditionally dated to 802 AD. At this time Jayavarman II was consecrated as devaraja or 'god who is king'.

The devaraja cult developed from worship of Shiva, symbolized by the linga, the phallic form of the god's creative force. The temple which was built to shelter the image of the god was a recreation of the celestials' mountain-top dwelling. Thus the most auspicious Khmer temples were either built on real mountains or as temple-mountains, which mimicked the natural form. Through the intermediary of the priest the ruler as earthly king could be united with his divine aspects.

The first of the Khmer devarajas, Jayavarman II, is thought to have returned to Cambodia about 800 AD from exile in Java (this is not necessarily the present island of Java!). After shifting his centre of power several times, he established his capital on Mount Mahendra. This has been identified as Phnom Kulen, located just north of Angkor. An inscription dated to 1052 AD from the temple of Sdok Kok Thom recounts that a priest or brahmin named Hiranyadama came to perform a ceremony that would make it impossible for Cambodia to continue to pay allegiance to Java. Jayavarman II, was consecrated sovereign, to be cakravartin or universal ruler.

Shiva linga, c.11th-12th century.

This ceremony marks the beginning of over six hundred years of Khmer expansion, lasting until 1431 when Angkor fell to the Thais. Jayavarman II's immediate successors ruled from the site of Roluos, located to the southeast of Angkor. The next ruler but one, Indravarman I (877-89), played a significant role in two key aspects of the Khmer state - the temple-mountain and water management. Building of both Preah Ko and Bakong were started at Roluos during Indravarman I's reign. The Bakong (881 AD) was Indravarman's devaraja shrine, whereas Preah Ko (879 AD) was dedicated to his predecessors. The Bakong stands upon a series of pyramidal terraces and culminates with a tower at the top. The inspiration for this plan is believed by some scholars to have come from the contemporary monument of Borobodur in Java. However, the lack of enclosure of the terraces which is such a vital part of Borobodur's plan, leaves this link open to question.

One of the oldest lintels found in Thailand is this example in the Thala Borivat style, dating from the first half of the 7th century. Its exact provenance is unknown, but it is now housed at Wat Supatnaram, Ubon Ratchathani province. Makaras on either side disgorge a double arch, linked by a central medallion. The makara's tapering bodies are a feature of the end of the Thala Borivat style in transistion to the following Sambor Prei Kuk period. The simha in the medallion is carved in a local style.

Khmer water management

Indravarman I also constructed the first of the large reservoirs or baray in the Angkorean plain, the Indratataka. While rectangular tanks both in the Angkor region and in Thailand predate this period, the Indratataka's scale epitomises the coordination of water management with the prosperity of the kingdom. The reservoir measures about 3,200 metres long and 750 metres wide. Indravarman I's successor, Yasovarman I (889-900 AD), constructed an even larger reservoir (7,120 x 1,700 metres). It is called the Yasodharatataka, and marked the foundation of his new capital at Yasodharapura, or Angkor.

The four corners of the reservoir were marked with inscriptions commemorating its consecration. Yasovarman likened the reservoir to the disk of the moon becoming water and reflecting like a mirror. He also called it the river of heaven. In Indian legends, the moon is the cup which holds the elixir of immortality. The body of water becomes a receptacle for the glory and power of the king, in the form of his store of the elixir. In this way the god who is king manifests his divinity.

The imagery of the reservoir as mirror also relates to the concept of the temple as microcosm of the universe. The world of the gods above contrasts with the primeval chaos of the world below. Harmony is achieved in the ordering of the temple, and the creation of huge reservoirs to act as mirrors. These become lenses to correct the reflection thereby harmonising it with the heavenly universe.

In this context, the reservoirs are religious constructions. Many scholars, however, view them as being part of a vast irrigation system which supported rice production for the people of Angkor. The reservoirs are seen as one element in an immense hydraulic system which also included supply channels, dykes, and field runnels to store fresh water, collect rain, and redistribute it to the ricefields.

The difficulty with this hypothesis is that there is no concrete evidence for such a system. Analysis of aerial photographs of the region shows a vast network, but the canals from the moats run within the city of Angkor, to other reservoirs, or to the moats surrounding temples. There is no corresponding set of feeder canals extending into the surrounding ricefields. It has been suggested that water seeped out under the dykes, but contemporary agronomists have shown this to be unlikely.

The construction of large reservoirs continued after Yasovarman I's time. In the 11th century, during the reigns of Suryavarman I and Udayadityavarman II, the West Baray was created, measuring 8,000 metres in length and 2,100 metres in width. The construction of the large baray at Muang Tam may date to this period. In the 12th century, Suryavarman II began construction of a reservoir in the southeast sector of the city measuring some 4,000 by 3,000 metres. Jayavarman VII, in the late 12th and early 13th centuries, was unable to surpass previous efforts, in part because the metropolis was already filled with temples and reservoirs and he was obliged to build over the surrounds of many earlier temples to place his temple, the Bayon, in the middle of the

Somasutra, Prasat Phu Prasat. (Ubon Rajathani Musuem).

city. To the north of the central area, he placed one of his ancestral temples, Preah Khan. Cardinally aligned with the monument was a reservoir, measuring some 3,400 by 800 metres.

Despite the size and number of these reservoirs, there is no record in inscriptions of their use for irrigation, or of disputes arising about water allocation. While Sanskrit inscriptions are chiefly poetic, such as Yasovarman's imagery of the reservoir, the Khmer inscriptions describe everyday life. They record the founding of villages, the duties of the peoples in the service of the temple, revenue requirements, and legal disputes. They speak of the amounts of rice required by the temples, and the allocation of ricefields, even including their names, such as 'Egg-plant ricefield'. The construction of tanks is also mentioned. However, the subjects of irrigation, or disputes arising from water rights, are conspicuously absent, and startlingly so, considering the great size of the reservoirs themselves.

Other lacunae cast doubt upon the irrigation hypothesis as well. Chou Ta-Kuan, a 13th century Chinese traveller to Angkor, recorded many aspects of life there. He mentions rice growing but is silent on any system of irrigation, which would have been of interest to him. It has been suggested that his lack of reference to irrigation stems from the fact that the empire was in decline by the end of the 13th century, in part because of a failure of the water management system. However, given the tone of the rest of Chou Ta-Kuan's report, such economic collapse would have been noted.

Finally, there are no ethnographic parallels elsewhere in Southeast Asia for a large scale centralized system of irrigation. Small-scale locally-managed systems of water control are, in contrast, seen across the region from northern Thailand to Bali. It must be remembered that Yasovarman deliberately chose to build at Angkor, and that this location proved advantageous for several hundred years. The building of the Bakong and Preah Ko temples, as well as the construction of the reservoir, were vast undertakings, and would not have been possible in an unproductive area. The water supply in the region of Angkor came from rivers flowing down from Mount Kulen, but also, and most significantly, from the waters of the Tonlé Sap, the great lake to the south of Angkor. During the rainy season the lake literally doubles in size. As the rains subside, the waters slowly retreat, allowing them to be retained by the reservoirs, and a system of earthen dikes which bordered the northern shore of the lake. Thus it would seem that then, as now, the agricultural productivity of the Angkorean region rested not upon a centralized system of irrigation but upon small-scale control of water in flood-retreat rice cultivation.

French periodization of Khmer art

The art and architecture of the Khmer has been classified into periods by French art historians. Each style takes its name from the principal monument built by the ruler at Angkor, with the sequence being based on a combination of epigraphical information, evolution of the temple-mountain concept, and types of ornamental carving. Many of the elements found on the Khmer doorway - pilasters, pediments, lintels, and colonettes - have been shown to change over the centuries and have come to be used as an index by which to date a temple. Lintels in particular have proved useful, as the large pieces of stone often survive even when the rest of the temple has collapsed.

There are fourteen stylistic periods, which can be divided into a pre-Angkorean (c.600 - c.800 AD), a Transitional (c.825-875 AD) and an Angkorean phase (c.875 - 1230). These are listed below along with some of the principal rulers.

PRE-ANGKOREAN		
1.Phnom Da	c. early 6th century	Bhavavarman I, Mahendravarman
2.Sambor Prei Kuk	c. 600-650	Isanavarman I
3. Prei Kmeng	c. 635-700	Bhavavarman II
4. Kompong Preah	c.706-825	
TRANSITIONAL		
5. Kulen	c. 825-875	Jayavarman II
ANGKOREAN		
6. Preah Ko	c.875-893	Indravarman I
7.Bakheng	c.893-925	Yasovarman I
8. Koh Ker	c.921-945	Jayavarman IV
9. Pre Rup	c.947-965	Rajendravarman II
10. Banteay Srei	c.967-1000	
11. Khleang	c.965-1010	Jayavarman V
12. Baphuon	c.1010-1080	Udayadityavarman II
13. Angkor Wat	c.1100-1175	Suryavarman II
14. Bayon	c.1177-1230	Jayavarman VII

Khmer temples in Thailand built during the ascendancy of the Angkorean capital are described using the same periodization. The usage is in part legitimate, as Khmer temples in Thailand and those in Cambodia derive from the same tradition and until recently, the bulk of the scholarship on Khmer art and architecture has been carried out by westerners, particularly the French. This situation came about due to the former French colonisation of Indochina, present-day Laos, Vietnam, and Cambodia.

Thailand, however, has never been a colony, and while traditions of art and archaeology in the early 20th century followed the western-derived models developed to explain the sequence of Khmer architecture in Cambodia, in recent years Thai scholarship has become increasingly independent. This trend at first affected the field of prehistory, but for historical periods as well, the material culture of Thailand is ill-served by derivative terminology. For example, in describing the unique appearance of a lintel from an 11th century Khmer temple in Thailand, the only vocabulary available to the Thai art historian at present takes its paradigms from Khmer temples in Cambodia. Consequently, the Thai must resort to detailing why the lintel is not like the prototype, leaving the impression that the 'best' works are to be found in Cambodia. The special qualities that exist only in Khmer works in Thailand are now being recognized, and it is likely that soon a new means of classifying Khmer art in Thailand will be created.

Angkorean period temples in Thailand

The majority of Khmer temples in Thailand were built after the 10th century. During the reign of Rajendravarman II (944-968AD), control was exerted over an increasing number of Northeastern Thai principalities. A few structures, such as Prasat Beng, can be attributed to this period, but all have been vandalized. It was a difficult time for the Khmer, and Rajendravarman II's predecessor, Jayavarman IV, had been forced to abandon Angkor. Rajendravarman II managed to re-establish the capital at Angkor, but also attempted to extend control to Champa, on the coast of southern Vietnam. His reign is also remembered in association with Banteay Srei, 'citadel of women', a small and beautifully carved red sandstone temple built by the king's chief priest.

A number of temples remain in Thailand from the 11th century, in the Khleang and Baphuon styles. Many are three brick towers on a single platform, such as Prasat Prang Ku in Sisaket province. Others, such as Ban Phluang in Surin province, have only one tower of sandstone and probably brick, on a laterite T-shaped base. A different plan dating to the same period is seen at Prasat Kamphaeng Yai in Sisaket province. Instead of a platform with multiple towers, the buildings of the sanctuary are aligned within a gallery. In the case of Prasat Muang Tam, another 11th century temple, there are two enclosures: an inner gallery and an outer laterite wall.

The Angkorean monarch during the first half of the 11th century was Suryavaman I. Although some control over the Northeastern parts of Thailand had existed in the previous century, Suryavarman I is credited with consolidating these gains. His reign is thought to have been a stable one, with conflicts with Champa dying down. Suryavarman I's successor was his son Udayadityavarman II. He ruled from 1050-1066 AD, during which time he continued to expand the Khmer-controlled domain. Revolts occurred in a number of locations, and a resurgence of battles with Champa weakened the kingdom. Udayadityavarman II nonetheless continued to build temples, and among these is the Baphuon. Although much of the temple has been destroyed, its plan may have served as a prototype for the temple of Angkor Wat built in the first half of the 12th century.

By the end of the 11th century in Thailand, sandstone was the main construction material, although brick was still used, as evidenced by the five brick towers of Prasat Sikhoraphum. During this period, the plan of some parts of the temple, particularly the central tower, became more elaborate. In addition to the square inner cell (garbhagrha), there was also a corridor (antarala) connecting this to the antechamber (mandapa). Sometimes the portal of the main door of the antechamber is elaborated with a shallow porch (ardhamandapa). Several examples of this plan remain, including Prasat Phimai and Prasat Phnom Wan, in Nakhon Ratchasima province and Prasat Phnom Rung in Buriram province .

Parts of these temples may have provided models for the construction of Angkor Wat by Suryavarman II (1113-1150). Angkor Wat was a massive undertaking, noted both for its plan and for the extensive reliefs carved on the walls of the gallery. These carvings are two metres high and continue for over 1,500 metres. The temple is unusual in being dedicated to the god Vishnu, and facing west. Neither practice appears to have been adopted by the Khmer in Thailand, with the exception of Prasat Bai Baek in Buriram province which faced west. However, the ritual associated with the temple is unclear.

The 12th century Angkor Wat temple, built by Suryavarman II and dedicated to Vishnu, is the epitome of Khmer architecture.

During the end of the 12th and early 13th centuries, the rate of Khmer temple building reached its height. A number of these were Mahayana Buddhist, the religion adopted by the ruler at Angkor, Jayavarman VII, (1181-1219 AD) who had come to the throne after a devastating Cham attack on the capital. He not only subdued the Chams, but revived the organization of the empire and was perhaps the most active of all the rulers at Angkor, leaving a large number of inscriptions. His great city, Angkor Thom, had at its centre the largest of all temple complexes, the Bayon. In was in this building that he declared visually his adherence to Mahayana Buddhism.

Many new shrines dedicated to Mahayana Bodhisattvas were built outside Angkor during Jayavarman VII's reign. In addition to temples in Northeast Thailand, structures were built in areas to the west and far north into the central plain of Thailand. While some, such as Wat Si Sawai in Sukhothai district, have been largely built over in later periods, others such as Muang Singh have recently been excavated by the Fine Arts Department and have disclosed an extensive city complex.

One specific type of laterite structure which is unique to Jayavarman VII's era is known as a hospital, as inscriptions found at many record dedications to a Mahayana Buddha associated with healing. Another small type of building erected at this time is called a rest house, for numbers of these appear to have acted as roadside sanctuaries on the provincial roads leading to the capital at Angkor.

Kings continued to rule at Angkor after Jayavarman VII. Chou Ta-Kuan's account is informative on the splendor of the court. The expansionary policies of Jayavarman VII, however, had seriously over-extended the resources of his empire. For the common people, his adoption of Mahayana Buddhism appears to have offered little change to their arduous lives.

The Thai kingdoms in the central plain grew increasingly strong, and eventually, in 1431, sacked Angkor. The Khmer heritage was not lost, for the motifs and

Syam kuk ('Siamese people') bas relief from the south gallery of Angkor Wat, late 12th century.

Prasat KamphaengYai. Restoration, 1990.

The west entrance to the central enclosure, Prasat Muang Singh, Kanchanaburi.

architecture of the Hindu and Mahayana Buddhist temples were incorporated into the religious structures of Sukhothai during the 13th to 15th century, although the Khmer temples themselves generally fell into disuse and were for many centuries left to crumble. Today many are being restored and venerated as part of Thailand's cultural heritage.

Restoration

The history of monumental restoration in Thailand owes much to the inventories of Etienne Aymonier and Lunet de Lajonquière, begun in the early 1900s. These works were later updated by Erik Seidenfaden, and in 1959 and 1960 by the Thai Fine Arts Department.

The establishment of the first governmental department charged with protection of monuments was due to the efforts of Prince Damrong Rajanubhab. Thailand's Archaeological Survey, founded in 1925, began clearing and preserving many of the monuments, as well as recording stone inscriptions. Many of the French scholars, notably George Cœdès, served as advisors to the archaeology division.

The French also played a major role in the first large scale restoration of a Khmer temple in Thailand, that undertaken at Phimai. B.P. Groslier, Director of Archaeological Research of the Ecole Francaise d'Extrême Orient, and Curator at Angkor, undertook a technical study of the temple in 1962. This was used by the Thai Fine Arts Department in their restoration work at Phimai between 1964 and 1969. Of particular value was the French expertise in the technique of anastylosis used so successfully at Angkor by B.P. Groslier. This method of reconstruction, adopted by the French at Angkor after its application by Dutch architects working in Java, consists of the rebuilding of a monument using both materials and construction methods appropriate to the specific monument. It sanctions the use of new materials, such as the making of new stone blocks, where needed in order to re-assemble the remaining ancient elements of the structure. Rather than simply replacing blocks which have fallen, anastylosis demands the complete disassembly of the monument. Each block is numbered, and the authenticity and correctness of each block assessed prior to its replacement on the monument.

Since its initial use at Phimai, anastylosis has been employed at all major reconstructions of Khmer temples in Thailand. The largest undertaking was at Prasat Phnom Rung, a seventeen year project begun in 1971. From 1972 to 1975, an American, Vance Childress, carried out a three year program of restoration at the 11th century temple of Prasat Ban Phluang, Surin. Since the completion of Prasat Phnom Rung in 1988, the Fine Arts Department has increased the pace and scope of Khmer reconstructions, with work at at Muang Singh, Kanchanaburi; Prasat Kamphaeng Yai, Sisaket; Muang Tam, Buriram; and Phnom Wan, Nakhon Ratchasima.

2 THE ART OF THE KHMER

ARCHITECTURE

Opposite
The central prang of Phnom Rung, 12th century.

The mountain is home of the gods in both Hindu and Buddhist cosmology. Mount Meru rises up from a central continent, and is surrounded by concentric rings of mountains and oceans. The Khmer temple recreates this cosmos in miniature. The central tower, often flanked by subsidiary ones, stood for the five peaks of the Mount, while the wall and surrounding moat symbolised the encircling mountains and waters. The temple complex was enclosed within a stone wall, often bordered by a further moat.

The Khmer did not develop the technique of true vaulting, and the restrictions imposed by the corbelled arch had important consequences architecturally. This lack of true vaulting meant that large areas could not be roofed over, but as assembly of the faithful was not an integral part of ritual, the stimulus to develop the true arch was not present. Instead Khmer architecture developed the use of multiple chapels, which, crowned with tiered roofs, were then joined with galleries. Thus the vertical thrust of the towers was balanced by a lateral expansion of galleried enclosures. In this way the development of the temple complex fulfilled its ritual function of establishing harmony through a microcosmic restructuring of the macrocosm.

The Central Tower

Although vast spaces were not desirable within the central tower of the Khmer temple, it was the tower and its supporting structure which received the greatest elaboration, in particular around the windows and doors. Each central cell generally had four entrances, oriented towards each cardinal direction, although in many of the smaller temples, only the principal entry is functional, with the other three being false doors.

The doorways are crowned with an arch, supported by pilasters and often ending in the upturned heads of nagas. Under the arch is the fronton or pediment, frequently carved with a Hindu or Buddhist scene. Within the frame of the arch and pediment, is a second framing made up of lintel and colonettes. Like the pediment, the lintels are principal vehicles for carving.

Structural and decorative lintels

The lintel was fitted to the jambs using a variety of techniques. Generally, this involved cutting a 45° degree triangular wedge out of the lintel, and inserting into it the positive element to match the form, carved from the top of the doorframe. By the 13th century, however, when it seems that many temples were constructed in a hurry, the lintel was often just laid flat on the doorjambs. These changed also, often being made up of a stack of stones, rather than a single stone such as seen at Muang Khaek.

An arch, or in later periods, a rectangle, was built of stone blocks on top of the structural lintel to prevent the weight of the building cracking the lintel. A second, decorative lintel with carving, was then fixed to the structural lintel. In the 11th and 12th century, this was usually done by removing a square section from the lower rear corner of the lintel, thereby creating an overhang, or hook, which allowed the decorative lintel to be hung on the front of the functional lintel. The structural member was also cut and hung so as to balance the additional weight of the decorative lintel.

Decorative lintels play a major role in Khmer architecture. The lintel was one of the principal areas for carving and as such is a rich source for iconographical study as well as an invaluable aid to dating based on carving style.

This technique had many variations, depending on the width of the lintel in relation to the rest of the doorframe. Sometimes the functional lintel even had a small lip on the front to accomodate the second lintel. The colonettes, which were placed in front of the doorjamb on both sides, served to support the front part of the decorative lintel. By the 13th century, many temples were being built of laterite blocks. These blocks were cut just after removing the stone from the ground, while the laterite was still soft. The laterite blocks are generally larger than sandstone blocks, which in turn affected methods of construction. For example, earlier brick buildings often had a stone cross-piece inserted midway up the facade. This allowed positioning of a stone pediment to complement the lower stone lintel without the danger of too much weight pressing down on the lintel and cracking it, as well as potentially collapsing the brick layers. The use of the very large laterite blocks by-passed this problem, since the weight of the upper pediment could be distributed across several substantial pieces.

This is the only known example of two-tone brick construction in Thailand. Prasat Bai Baek, 11th century.

Construction materials

Brick, sandstone and laterite were the three principal structural materials used in Khmer architecture. The predominance of one over the others varied according to the needs of a particular structure and the local availability. Most Khmer builders prior to the 9th century preferred brick to stone, but by the end of the century sandstone began to replace brick construction. However, even after sandstone began to predominate during the second half of the 11th century, brick was still seen in a number of structures. During the entire span of Khmer architecture up to the 13th

The partially collapsed door of the north prang of Prasat Yai Ngao illustrates that, while not the predominant material, brick was still being used in the 12th century. Sandstone was used where carving was required and for important structural elements such as windows and door frames.

century, wood was used for all non-religious buildings, and for ceilings, stiffening elements, and frameworks in stone structures.

When brick was the primary material, it was assembled without mortar by means of a flexible substance of vegetable origin. In addition, the bricks were rubbed together, grinding them and rendering the joinery almost imperceptible. Mouldings and profiles were carved after the brick was placed. Figures were sculpted, and a series of holes made to later receive and hold a coating.

The use of brick to build Khmer towers in Northeast Thailand dates to the earliest monuments, such as the 7-8th century Prasat Phumphon, in Surin province. These are preceded in Cambodia by the brick buildings at Sambor Prei Kuk. The popularity of brick continued throughout the span of Khmer temple construction. By the 11th century, a number of brick monuments were erected, such as Prasat Muang Tam and Prasat Kamphaeng Yai. Although these were no different from earlier structures in their basic designs, development was seen in an increasing degree of rebatement, and a greater articulation of the pedimental areas over doorways. By the 12th century, as is the case at Prasat Sikhoraphum, the brick pediment creates a shallow porch on the front of the building.

From the end of the 10th century, progress in methods of stone construction meant that brick was reserved for secondary buildings or elements such as vaults or arches not yet built in sandstone. Stone, however, was never absent in any brick construction. It was used for foundations and platforms, while certain other constructional elements were also in sandstone such as structural lintels and thresholds, although these would sometimes employ laterite for reasons of economy in regions far from sandstone quarries.

Laterite was the commonest material available, and was used in all eras, for big works, basements, and thick walls. Particularly during the late 12th century reign of Jayavarman VII, the rate of building increased. With such hasty construction, laterite was seen everywhere, covering vaults, in non-sculptured parts of walls, secondary edifices, and provincial foundations. As in brick buildings, however, sandstone continued to be used for areas of detailed carving.

Given its adaptability, sandstone was often carved in imitation of wood, not always an effective application. Mortar was not used, the blocks being ground together to produce a structure held together mainly by inertia. Iron was frequently used as a safeguard, incisions being carved horizontally in the two sandstone pieces so that they could be secured by a metal pin.

Two stages in the preparation of sandstone blocks from the enclosure wall at Phnom Rung. The left hand example showing the unhoned front surface, while at right they are fully dressed and prepared.

Carved friezes from just above the base of the sanctuary tower at Phimai (above) and from beneath the cornice of the gallery at Phnom Rung (below). It should be noted that when such friezes are used on the lower parts of a building the petal shapes point upwards, whereas when used on the upper parts they point downwards. Early 12th century.

Friezes from above and below a window show a variety of floral motifs.

A corner from a false window frame at Muang Tam, showing the use of a mortice joint, a technique borrowed from carpentry although it was totally unnecessary in stone carving.

False door from Ku Suan Taeng, early 13th century. Note the deep projecting stone slab at the top used to support the pediment, which due to changes in architectural techniques could no longer be carried by the decorative lintel.

In the 13th century laterite was widely used both in new construction and additions to existing temples, such as in this false window from the laterite gallery at Phnom Rung.

Of unknown origin, this incomplete 8th century lintel in the Kompong Preah style is the only such example known in Thailand. That it has been cut into three sections, of which the central one is missing, suggests that it was stolen, possibly even from an as-yet-undiscovered temple along the Thai-Cambodian border. The central motif is likely to have been floral, as in the apparently similar lintel from Prasat Bhumprasat in Cambodia.

Featuring Vishnu riding Garuda, who holds the tails of two triple-headed nagas, this lintel from Prachinburi is traditionally dated to the mid-10th century Pre Rup period, although a number of Bakheng-style features (the outward facing nagas, Garuda and garlands) make the dating uncertain.

By the second half of the 9th century, the kala appears as the central motif disgorging garlands from sides of its mouth. This and the outward facing makaras at either end are characteristic of the Preah Ko style. This lintel from Sathan Phra Narai in Nakhon Ratchasima province dates from the end of this period. The slightly stiff quality in the carving may be a feature of local workmanship.

Carvings and artefacts from the 11th century Baphuon period are the most widely found in Thailand. In this lintel from Prasat Pako, Nakhon Ratchasima province, Indra riding the three-headed elephant Airavata has taken the place of the kala motif seen opposite. The two simhas clutching garlands on either side of the god are an unusal iconographic feature for this period.

Arranged in two tiers with a central motif of the god Vishnu riding Garuda, this lintel from Prang Ku, Sisaket province dates to the early Angkor Wat period around the beginning of the 12th century. Schematic nagas separate the two portions of the lintel, whose upper part has a row of dancing deities. While Vishnu's clothing and ornaments are in the Angkor Wat style, the garlands being disgorged by the simhas are in the earlier Baphuon style. The presence of two styles in one piece is a common occurence in Khmer carving in Thailand.

Another decorative element shown here has sometimes been mistaken for a lintel. In fact, friezes such as this featuring divinities were probably used in temple chapels for votive offerings.

An unfinished lintel from Muang Tam shows the preparatory stage for decorative carving. Perhaps the diamond shape in the middle was intended a kala.

Pilasters were generally carved with floral motifs arranged in a repetitive pattern. Muang Tam, 11th century.

Opposite
Phimai, early 12th century.

Pilaster detail, mandapa entrance, Phimai.

Pilaster detail Gopura III, Preah Vihear. (11th century)

Two of the earliest colonettes in Thailand are these Prei Kmeng style (c.635-c.700) examples, from Wat Keng Koi and now in the Ubon museum. The tops are decorated with lotus petals, floral pendants, garlands and representations of pearls in the Indian Gupta style that was the major influence in this period.

By the 11th and 12th centuries, the colonette had evolved considerably. It was now octagonal in section and the motifs were smaller and more stylised. At left, is an 11th century colonette from Muang Tam and, at right, a 12th century colonette from Sikhoraphum.

From the 10th century onwards pediments shared equal importance with lintels in Khmer architecture in providing an important area for decorative carving and the development of Khmer iconography. In almost all cases, the pediment is framed by two undulating naga bodies whose heads rear up to form the pediment ends.

This incomplete example found in Nang Rong district of Buriram, dates from the late 10th century.

The bald-headed naga from a pediment end from Muang Tam spews forth a floral pendant and dates from the 11th century.

The naga from one of the pediment ends at Phnom Rung, early 12th century, is characterized by the crown on its head.

All the parts which made up a Khmer sanctuary were provided with windows, both false and real, and all were ornamented with balusters, whose forms were probably originally inspired by bamboo poles. The carving style evolved over different periods becoming more elaborate with time. All three shown here date from the 11th and 12th centuries.

Balustred window, Phnom Wan.

False door from the south side of the sanctuary at Narai Jaeng Waeng, 11th century. Small prasats such as this one would only have had one entrance. On the three other sides were false doors with infills carved to imitate the wooden panels used to close the real door.

Balustred window, Phnom Rung.

Balustred window.

Overleaf
East entrance gopura and cross-shaped terrace with naga balustrades, Phnom Rung.

Sculpture in stone

The Khmer mastery of stone included three dimensional scuplture as well as the bas-reliefs which decorated the temples. The central shrine of the complex housed the cult image, generally carved from stone. The stylistic evolution of these images follows the same classification scheme as the temple architecture. However, whereas temples are often dated by the floral motifs of the lintels, hairstyle and dress provide the principal means of dating sculpture.

The Khmer stone carver performed a similar task whether working on a lintel bas-relief or a sculpture in the round - in essence a similar technique to wood carving, a tradition which long preceded the use of stone. Few pieces of stone sculpture dating from the pre-Angkorean period have been found in Thailand and most of the pieces found date from the 10th century onwards.

Bronzes

Khmer bronze work presents itself differently from stone sculpture both in its execution and use. The production of a lost-wax bronze involved a process of modelling rather than carving. In this regard, bronze casting presents affinities to stucco and terracotta modelling. The virtuosity of the Mon peoples of Central and Northeastern Thailand in modelling these materials suggests Khmer interaction with the Mon throughout the period of Khmer stone temple building.

The majority of bronze objects produced by the Khmer were part of a portable set of ritual objects. This very portability has made it difficult to provenance bronzes.

In comparison with finds of stone scuplture, a great deal of pre-Angkorean bronze images have been found in Thailand. Most are Mahayana Buddhistic images such as Buddhas and Bodhisattvas. Surprisingly, bronzes from the 10th and 11th centuries are scarce and the next important finds date to the 12th and through to the second half of the 13th century.

Fragments of a Buddha seated on naga, Baphuon period, 11th century. This image was found at Wat Mahathat, Ayutthaya but originated from another location. The head of the Buddha shows that it was carved in the 11th century. His chin is incised, his head bulges somewhat at the side; his hair is made up of curls giving a plaited impression. The upper part of the head (the ushnisha) is conical in shape decorated with strands of hair randomly placed and creating a subtle juxtaposition between the upper and lower parts of his hair. Even though his eyes stare straight ahead, his smiling mouth makes the image less severe and unusually attractive. The heads of the nagas at the side are turned to look up at the central head, now missing, which would originally have been looking upwards.

Buddha seated on naga, Angkor Wat style, 12th century. This immage was brought to the National Museum Bangkok from Wat Na Phra Men at Ayutthaya. It is a fully ornamented Buddha with an intricately carved head-dress. His ushnisha is cone-shaped decorated with lotus petals. The carver has suggested his monastic robe by means of a few light incisions. In addition, between the left arm and the body the carver has pierced the stone. Various explanations have been proposed as to why this was done. Some believe that the carver simply made a mistake, but as many such versions exist, this theory would seem unlikely. It may have been done to create the impression of an irradiating Buddha, whose inner radiance would have rendered his robe transparent.

Standing Buddha image in the abhaya position, Lopburi style, beginning to mid-13th century. This stone standing Buddha was moved from Wat Na Phra Men, Ayutthaya to Bangkok. No doubt it was previously at another location. Standing Buddhas of this period wear a belt decorated with flowers. The hem of his antaravasaka is also beautifully decorated. His hand in the abhaya gesture is close to his body instead of jutting out and this shows the influence of Pala art from India. This characteristic may also be seen in the Buddha image in an arch at Wat Ku Kut in Lamphun district from the late Dvaravati period which shows the influence both of Pala and Lopburi. (National Museum, Bangkok)

Stone Buddha image in meditation posture from Wat Phra Sri Ratana Mahathat, Lopburi, mid-13th century. This Buddha represents a true synthesis of Angkorean Khmer and local Lopburi Khmer styles. The treatment of the eyes is rather stiff and hard, reminiscent of the representation of Angkorean deities, but the emphasis on the edge of the lips is something not found in Bayon sculpture.

Left *Head of a door guardian, post-Bayon period, second half of the 13th century. This head illustrates how the Bayon influence continued after the official end of the period and its adaptation at the hands of local craftsmen. (Khonkaen Museum)*

Centre *A four-armed stone deity, late Baphuon style, end of the 11th century from Ku Noi, Na Doon district, Maha Sarakam province. Ku Noi is a Khmer site which would seem to date from the Baphuon period and is a single sandstone prasat surrounded by walls with an eastern and western gopura. A four-armed stone deity was found here but as the head, arms, and feet were all broken it has been impossible to establish its identity. However, the sampot worn by the figure dates from the late Baphuon period typified by its meticulous carving. (Khonkaen Museum)*

Opposite
Stone guardian, Angkor Wat style, 12th century from Ku Noi. The guardian figure, which has a third eye on his forehead and was holding a club which has been broken, seems to date from the end of the Angkor Wat period judging by the style of his sampot. However his belt is still in the Baphuon style as is his head-dress, which follows the old method used in that period in being tied at the back. Judging from the statue's smiling expression and the presence of a third eye on his forehead, the figure could well represent Nandikesvara. (Khonkaen Museum)

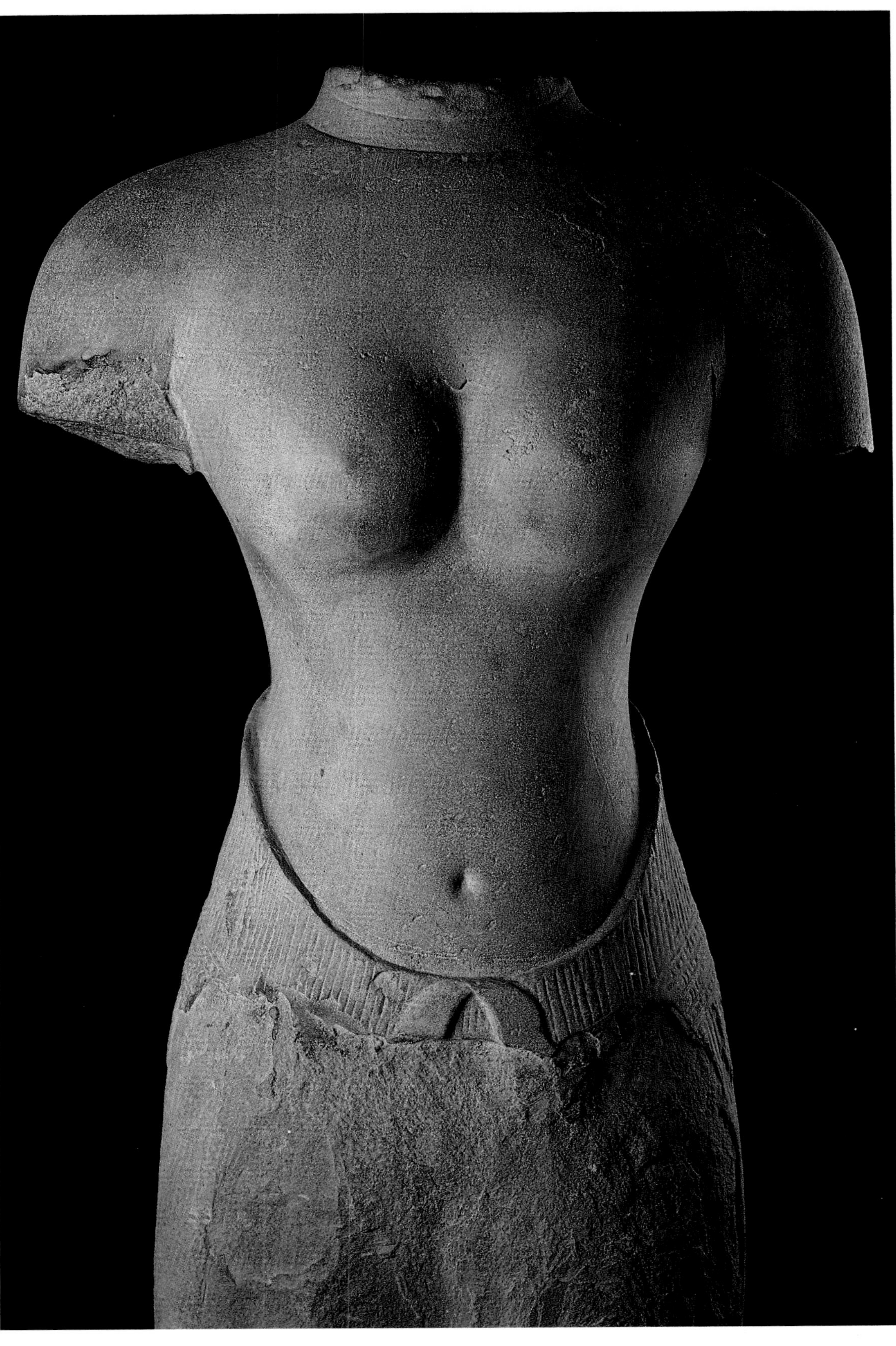

Female deity, Baphuon style, 11th century? Exactly who this statue represents is virtually impossible to identify as the head and arms are missing. In addition, accurate dating is difficult as the sampot is damaged. However, as the back of this garment is relatively high, while the front is beneath the navel, it would seem to date the statue to the Baphuon period. (National Museum, Bangkok)

*Bronze Buddha image protected by naga, 13th century. Stone images of the same subject during this period are unadorned, in contrast to bronzes such as this dressed in royal attire with jewellery and a crown.
The diadem of this particular bronze shows some Pala influence, while the monastic robe is in the Angkor Wat style and treated in a similar manner to certain stone images (see page 64) reinforcing the theory that the gap between the left arm and the body was a deliberate stylistic device.*

Left *An image of the divine architect, Vishvakarma, 13th century. Vishvakarma was the architect of the God Indra according to Buddhist tradition. He did not appear in Khmer iconography before the 12th century.*

Right *An unidentified divinity, probably Buddhist, in the Bayon style, 13th century. During the 12th and 13th centuries such small, religous bronzes became extremely popular. (National Museum, Bangkok)*

Meditating bronze Buddha, 13th century. This adorned Buddha image wears a monastic robe with the right shoulder bare and a space between his body and left arm (where one would have expected the folds of the robe to fall). A small conical object is held in the palm of his right hand. Perhaps this image represents Bhaisajyaguru, the Buddha who is associated with medicine. (National Museum, Bangkok)

Bronze Buddha image from the second half of the 13th century, showing the Pala influence in the subduing mara gesture and the style of the head-dress and earrings. This influence during this period might have reached Thailand via Pagan. (National Museum, Bangkok)

Prajñaparamita bronze, 13th century. This Prajñaparamita is recognisable by the lotus in her right hand, while her left would originally have held a book. Other elements are uncharacteristic. Instead of having a Buddha image in front of her chignon, she wears a head-dress and jewellery more reminiscent of the apsaras from the Angkor Wat and Bayon period. (National Museum, Bangkok)

Bronze ceremonial utensil with a Vajrasattva, 13th century. This piece shows the highly developed bronze casting techniques of the period with intricate detail in the floral design in which divinity figures are intertwined. The main figure is Vajrasattva, one of the important Mahayana Boddhisattvas. Above him is a small Buddha protected by naga.

Bronze dancers, 12th century. This piece is probably part of a pedestal. Although only two figures remain there may well have been more. Both are dressed in Angkor Wat style and convey an impression of lively movement. (National Museum, Bangkok)

A fragment from a bronze pedestal decorated with a scene probably from one of the great Hindu epics. 12th or 13th century.

A ceremonial drum with upper and lower parts of bronze. The top part is a vajra surrounded by figures in the anchalee position, while the lower part comprises four bronze Garudas supporting the drum. The drum itself, the wooden top fixture and the handle have been completely remade in the Bangkok period. The bronze parts date to the 13th century.

Top right
A broken bronze conch shell, 13th century. This shell is decorated with a dancing Hevajra, an important Bodhisattva in Mahayana Buddhism. (Khonkaen Museum)

Bottom right
Bronze conch on a stand composed of Garudas supported by nagas, 13th century. Conch shells were ritual objects over many centuries. Examples of actual shells and ceramic versions have been found, but in the 13th century bronze conches seem to have been the most popular ritual objects which have been found in significant numbers. The upper part would have been decorated with religious motifs which were generally Buddhist - Bodhisattvas or vajras.

Four-armed bronze Vishnu riding on the shoulders of a Garuda, 12th century. As well as supporting Vishnu, the Garuda's raised arms hold nagas. The action of stepping forward is unusual. Only two of Vishnu's attributes are recognisable - the conch shell in his upper left hand and the discus in his upper right hand.

Ceramics

The temples of the Khmer required a steady supply of ritual containers. The upper classes also needed vessels to store items such as honey, wine, and the lime used to make up the betel-chewing quid. While metal containers were prized the bronze-casting foundries have not been found; this despite many bronze statues thought to have been cast in Northeast Thailand. However ceramic vessels were also used. Excavations by the Fine Arts Department in recent years have shown that the area to the south of Prasat Phnom Rung and Prasat Muang Tam was a major ceramic-producing centre. Indeed, the extent of production suggests that Khmer ceramics made in Thailand were exported to all parts of the empire.

The pottery tradition of Northeast Thailand stretches back to the prehistoric era with, for example, the red-painted designs found in the cemeteries of Ban Chiang. Similar red painted wares have been found at settlements in the province of Muang Tam and Phnom Rung. Simple kilns dating to the early first millennium AD producing unglazed pottery have been excavated by archaeologists from Silapakorn University. Finally, numerous multi-chambered kilns such as those at Ban Kruat exist which were the production centres for the green and brown glazed ceramics used by the Khmer. Thus for thousands of years, the people of the Northeast have developed an expertise in making pots.

Household goods in the Khmer period were often fashioned in the shape of different animals. Elephants were extremely popular and were used in utensils of all sizes. A great many examples have been found at the Ban Kruat kilns. This elephant head is part of a brown ceramic jar and dates to the 12th or 13th century. Other animals are also found such as bears and frogs, and in addition human faces were frequently modelled.

Khmer kilns, Ban Kruat, after recent excavations by the Fine Arts Department.

Right and below
Two ceramic jars, 13th century. These two Khmer jars covered with a brown glaze were found at Nakhon Champasri, Na Doon district, Maha Sarakam province. Such jars are generally found in sites which have had Khmer influence and usually have the brown glaze seen here. The largest kilns were situated in Ban Kruat district and Ban Baranae in Laharnsai district, both in Buriram province. (Khonkaen Museum)

*Jug in the form of an elephant with a brown glaze, 13th century. Household goods in the Khmer period were often fashioned in the shape of different animals. Elephants were extremely popular and were used in utensils both small and middle size.
A great many examples have been found at the Ban Kruat kilns in Buriram.
(National Museum, Bangkok)*

Khmer ceramic jar, 13th century. Like the other two jars shown here, this is a brown glazed pot. Khmer glazes were very thin and if exposed to damp could easily flake off. (Ubon Museum)

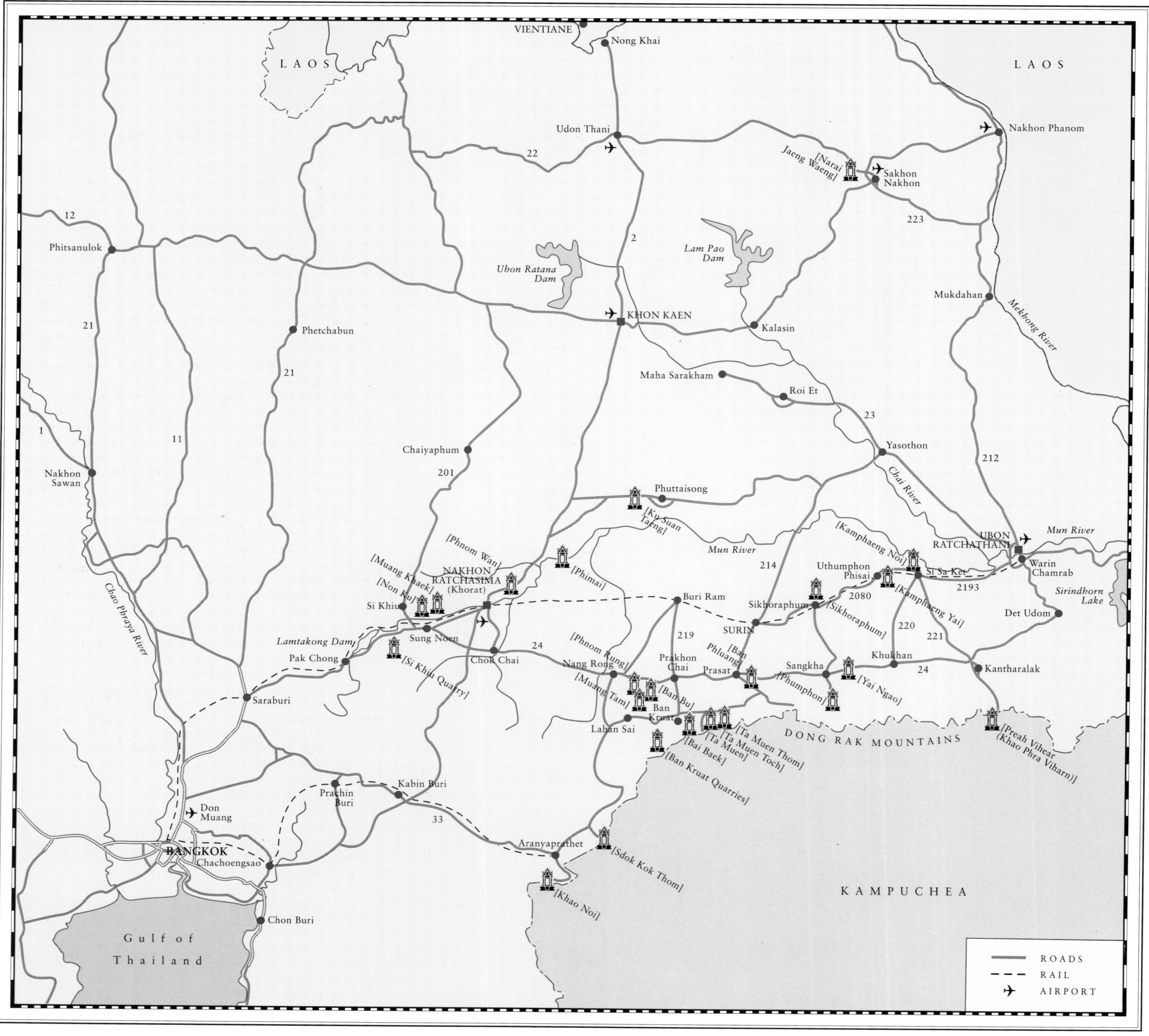
VIENTIANE
Nong Khai
LAOS
LAOS
Udon Thani
Nakhon Phanom
[Narai Jaeng Waeng]
Sakhon Nakhon
22
12
223
Phitsanulok
2
Lam Pao Dam
Ubon Ratana Dam
Mukdahan
KHON KAEN
Kalasin
Mekhong River
21
Phetchabun
21
Maha Sarakham
Roi Et
23
1
11
Yasothon
Chaiyaphum
212
Nakhon Sawan
201
Phuttaisong
Chai River
[Ku Suan Taeng]
[Kamphaeng Noi]
UBON RATCHATHANI
Mun River
Mun River
[Phnom Wan]
Warin Chamrab
Chao Phraya River
[Muang Khaek]
NAKHON RATCHASIMA (Khorat)
[Phimai]
214
Uthumphon Phisai
Si Sa Ket
2193
Sirindhorn Lake
[Non Ku]
2080
[Kamphaeng Yai]
Si Khiu
Buri Ram
Sikhoraphum
[Sikhoraphum]
Det Udom
SURIN
220
221
Lamtakong Dam
Sung Noen
219
[Phnom Rung]
24
[Ban Phluang]
Khukhan
Pak Chong
Chok Chai
Prakhon Chai
Nang Rong
Prasat
Sangkha
24
Kantharalak
[Si Khiu Quarry]
[Muang Tam]
[Ban Bu]
[Phumphon]
[Yai Ngao]
Saraburi
Ban Kruat
Lahan Sai
DONG RAK MOUNTAINS
[Ta Muen Thom]
[Ta Muen Toch]
[Ta Muen]
[Bai Baek]
[Preah Vihear (Khao Phra Viharn)]
[Ban Kruat Quarries]
Prachin Buri
Kabin Buri
Don Muang
33
Aranyaprathet
BANGKOK
Chachoengsao
[Sdok Kok Thom]
[Khao Noi]
KAMPUCHEA
Chon Buri
Gulf of Thailand
ROADS
RAIL
AIRPORT

3 THE TEMPLES

Opposite
Map of the Northeast of Thailand showing the location of the major Khmer temples.

Since the first surveys by Etienne Aymonier and Lunet de Lajonquière, some 300 Khmer sites have been discovered in Thailand, dating from the 7th to the 13th centuries. Most are in the southern part of the Khorat plateau in Northeast Thailand, which was Upper Cambodia during the time of the Khmer empire. A few other sites have been found in the north, in the west as far as Three Pagodas Pass on the Burmese border and in the Chao Phraya valley. However, most of the sites outside the Northeast have undergone constant renovation and are now substantially different from their original state. The relative isolation and, until recently, lack of development on the Khorat plateau have helped to preserve much of the original architecture intact.Thus this book concentrates on all the major sites which are architecturally sound and have extant buildings.

Until recently these sites have been overshadowed by the extensive work done by the French in Cambodia, and in particular at Angkor. It is only within the past 30 years that substantial excavation and restoration has been carried out in Thailand and the true importance of its Khmer temples is now acknowledged. The turning point was the careful restoration of Phimai and Phnom Rung beginning in the 1970s. Indeed, Phimai is one of the largest Khmer sanctuaries ever built, while the architectural decoration of Phnom Rung is widely considered to be some of the finest and innovative ever produced. Even more recent excavations and lesser known sites have uncovered remarkable bronze artefacts, including the largest complete Khmer cast figure ever found.

Finally, the discovery of many inscriptions has reinforced the important role of this region in the dynastic succession of the empire. The Northeast provided the Khmer empire with a line of kings that included two of its greatest rulers - Suryavarman II and Jayavarman VII.

PRASAT KHAO NOI

ปราสาทเขาน้อย

Opposite
Detail from the southern lintel of the northern prang.

Above
This shattered linga and its base were found in the vicinity of Khao Noi and then reassembled as far as possible. Judging from the force with which it was fractured, perhaps this site was intentionally destroyed, but whether as a result of war or a change in religious beliefs is not known.

This small prasat is situated in Prachinburi province and has recently undergone extensive renovation by the Fine Arts Department. Its main significance lies in its finely carved lintels which are among the earliest examples of Khmer carvings found in Thailand.

Built on an isolated hill, overlooking the western plains of Cambodia, its three brick prangs face east and are constructed in a row with the northern and middle prang on one base and the southern prang on a separate one. Following excavation the lintels are now housed in Prachinburi museum. Recently, the central prang has been rebuilt by the Fine Arts Department and copies of the lintels placed *in situ*. Although judging by these lintels, the prasat appears to have been built in the mid-7th century at the time of the Sambor Prei Kuk (c.600-c.650) and the beginning of the Prei Kmeng (c.635-c.700) periods (both overlap artisitically), the central prang was clearly reconstructed in the 11th century and the lintels from the original 7th century structure were reused.

This lintel dating from the 7th century and in the Sambor Prei Kuk style was reused on the middle prang, and may have come from its collapsed predecessor. While many characteristics are similar to those exhibited at Prasat Sambor Prei Kuk S7, there are also differences. The four arches which are being spewed out by the makaras at Sambor Prei Kuk are of equal size, while here the inner arches are significantly wider than the outer two. The figures inside the medallions connecting the arches are here only the vehicles of the gods - an elephant in the centre and horses in the outer two. At Sambor Prei Kuk, the gods themselves are portrayed on their vehicles.

The southern lintel (top) and the northern lintel (bottom) from the northern prang show great similarities in their Sambar Prei Kuk style and iconography. Thus makaras on either side face inwards and disgorge a series of arches connected by medallions. The principal difference is that in the northern lintel, Indra rides the elephant Airavata in the centre flanked by Asvins on their horses, while in the southern lintel the hamsa (the sacred goose, seen elsewhere at the site) makes an appearance.

This eastern lintel from the northern prang was carved in early Prei Kmeng style. The stylistic evolution from the Sambor Prei Kuk manner may be seen firstly, in the replacement of the makaras with praying figures, whose hairstyle of tight curls has not been found on any other lintel of this period whether in Thailand or Cambodia. Secondly, the looped arches of the earlier lintels have now become a single arch, although the medallions remain in place.

The western lintel from the northern prang is also in the Prei Kmeng style, although lacking the fluidity of the eastern lintel. Indeed, it is reminiscent of the lintel from Prasat Robang Romeah (E) in Cambodia in having five medaillions. Incompletely carved simhas flank the central arch, while the five medallions enclose hamsas. Such iconographic combinations have not been found in Cambodia.

PRASAT PHUMPHON

ปราสาทพูมโพน

Top
The lintel from above the eastern door of the large prang has been destroyed long ago but remnants of carving remain attached to the building at the top. The swirling foliage shows the influence of Gupta and post-Gupta periods which was pervasive in Asia at that time. The simha or lion with a bird-like head, although badly damaged, is reminiscent of a Banaspati beast in Dvaravati art.

Above
The door frame of the small prang to the north of the large prang is structurally interesting. Firstly, the functional lintel is mounted by a 45°degree angle mitred joint, a type of construction which is most unusual for a pre-Angkorean structure (except for certain sites such as Prasat A at Han Chei, Cambodia, which would seem to be the oldest prasat using such a joint). Normally the lintels would rest in a right-angle joint carved out of the door supports, reinforced by a stone spur. Secondly, the door colonettes and the door jambs are carved from a single piece, a technique that was not generally used elsewhere until the latter part of the Angkorean period.

Prasat Phumphon, or Banteai Phum Pon as referred to by de Lajonquière is situated in the Sangkha district of Surin. Built in the 7th century in the Prei Kmeng style, it is the oldest known Khmer structure in Thailand in good condition.

It is made up of four structures facing east and sited on a north-south axis. Today only one building remains in a relatively complete condition. Its brick structure is built to a square plan common to pre-Angkorean structures and measures about 5.7 metres on each side. The corners of this building have pilasters attached to the walls, while the false entrances above the side walls are each topped by a miniature replica building instead of the more usual portico. The roof is stepped and would probably have been decorated with a replica building on the corners of each level facing in each cardinal direction. Inside, traces remain of the red paint which would originally have decorated the interior. In addition, in the four corners we can see the holes which would have supported the columns of the interior mandapa. This building is constructed on the same base as another small brick building to its north, of which all that remains is the door frame.

To the south of the large prang is a square laterite base which probably originally supported an open wooden pavilion with a tiled roof. Approximately 30 metres to the north of the main tower are the remains of another rectangular brick structure. A fine lintel has been found here, together with the columns of this building. These, currently housed in the National Museum, Bangkok, offer the primary means of dating the structure.

Below
In this lintel the makaras of earlier periods, such as at Khao Noi, have disappeared, announcing the new Prei Kmeng style. Nevertheless, the presence of four small arches recalls the earlier Sambor Prei Kuk period.
(National Museum, Bangkok)
Photo: Mark Williams.

PRASAT NON KU

ปราสาทโนนกู่

Opposite
Door frames of the east gopura stand silhouetted against a stormy sunset.

Situated in the Soong Nern district of Nakhon Ratchasima province, the neighbouring 10th century temples of Prasat Non Ku and Muang Khaek are thought to have been the religious centres of the ancient city of Muang Khorakhapura. Constructed during the Koh Ker period, Prasat Non Ku's outer wall encloses a small square temple on a sandstone base which faces east and two smaller shrines which face west. Muang Khaek and Non Ku, located about 30 kilometres west of the present provincial capital, occupy a strategic defensive and trade position on the western edge of the Northeast's Khorat Plateau.

In this region, many streams flow down from the hills which mark the boundary of the plateau. Just to the northeast of Phimai, these tributaries merge into the Mun River. The Mun continues east across the plateau, finally emptying into the Mekong River across the Laotian border. The presence of many streams on the upper reaches of the Mun has meant that alluvium has been deposited, creating one of the most fertile areas on the plateau. It is an area with abundant salt, a product that inscriptions mention was transported by boat. Muang Khorakhapura was also near to the present town of Si Khiu, where fine sandstone quarries were found. That these combined advantages were apparent to the ancient Khmer is clearly seen in the cluster of temples which were founded in this area - Phimai, Phnom Wan, along with Non Ku and Muang Khaek are well placed to utilise the waterways of the upper Mun. During at least part of its existence, Muang Khorakhapura shared this area with another large city, the 9th-11th century Muang Sema. Some scholars think that Muang Sema was the centre of a kingdom recorded in inscriptions as Sri Chanasa. Unlike the Hindu remains found at Muang Khorakhapura, Muang Sema's rulers are thought to have been Buddhist.

Prasat Non Ku was included in the inventories carried out by both Aymonier and de Lajonquière. Subsequently 1959 saw the first excavations and restorations carried out at this site by the Fine Arts Department. The work was incomplete and recently the Department has carried out additional works. The tower which was constructed on a sandstone base has completely collapsed, all that remains being the two-metre high rectangular base. Various artefacts found in the vicinity lead to a date within the Koh Ker period or at least to the first half of the 10th century.

A demon-faced sandstone guardian from Non Ku holds a spear in his right hand and a lotus flower in his left. His head-dress is made up of a tiara, his hair forms a pointed spiral and he wears large round earrings. From these attributes we can conclude that this guardian is a Mahakala who is normally paired with a human-faced guardian known as Nandikesvara. And indeed the latter figure was discovered during excavations but in a damaged condition. It is difficult to determine where these figures were originally placed - whether they were set into the walls of the building or used as roof ornaments. (Mahavirawong Museum, Khorat)

This Garuda antefix, similar to antefixes found at neighbouring Muang Khaek, would have been one of the roof ornaments decorating the cornice level of the now-collapsed prasat. (Mahavirawong Museum, Khorat)

At the front of the prasat are two structures: one to the north, in the foreground, and one to the south. Both are built of brick on a sandstone base and their west-facing entrances suggest that both were what are commonly referred to as 'libraries'. Brick had been used for architecture in Cambodia since the sixth century AD. Where extra strength was required, such as in the base of structures, easily-available laterite would generally be used. However, at Non Ku sandstone also played a large part in the construction of the base of the building, over and above the used of stone in the door frames. Such abundant use of sandstone appears extravagant, but may have been necessary to prevent the walls from splaying. The base of the main prang is extremely high and, although it is not in the form of a stepped pyramid, it is particularly characteristic of this period of Khmer architecture.

PRASAT MUANG KHAEK

ปราสาทเมืองแขก

Opposite
The main prang from the south-east. The high base has been extended by wings to the east and west, which may have been intended for two small buildings which were never built.

Right
These antefixes would have been used as roof decorations, normally appearing at cornice level in the corner angles, while the corners themselves would have been decorated with miniature buildings. The figures carved onto these antefixes are (from top to bottom) a dancing deity, a praying rishi and a dikpalaka. (Mahavirawong Museum, Khorat)

Prasat Muang Khaek , situated in the Soong Nern district of Nakhon Ratchasima province, dates from the end of the Koh Ker period, c. 940 AD. Today, only the sandstone features, notably the door frames of the central sanctuary and northern gopura, are standing. Three massive pieces of sandstone make up each doorframe, with the structural lintels overhanging the doorjambs. Originally, these would have had additional support from the walls.

Recent excavations by the Fine Arts Department have greatly increased our knowledge of the site. We now know that this site embodies the same constructional principles and plan as those found at Prasat Thom of the same period in Cambodia, 100 miles north-east of Angkor, in which outer structures are large and gradually diminish in size towards the centre of the temple. However, at Prasat Thom the mandapa can only be entered from the front, whereas at Muang Khaek entry can also be effected from the two sides. This style of architecture is reminiscent of the Chola style in India which covered the period 900-1287 AD.

The main prang was built from brick on a relatively high sandstone base, and, although the walls and roof have collapsed long ago, it is still possible to appreciate its rather unusual nature; both the northern entrance to the mandapa and the doorway connecting the mandapa to the antarala are much taller and larger than the side entrances. Although all the brick walls have disappeared, we can surmise that the roof would also probably have been brick.

This Koh Ker style lintel showing a deity sitting above a kirtimukha was discovered during the recent excavations at Muang Khaek. It is almost complete, except for the upper corners which were left unfinished and is extremely fine when compared with other lintels from the same site. It is very close in style to its Cambodian models. Interestingly, the kala also shows elements of the earlier Preah Ko style (c.875-893AD). (Phimai Museum)

Lintel showing Vishnu Vamanavatara, Koh Ker style, c.940 AD. Iconographically this is one of the finest lintels from Muang Khaek. The middle section shows Vishnu stepping out in a most lifelike manner, a very naturalistic pose which is at odds with the rather stiff representation of the garland and foliage. The hamsas perched on the garland and flapping their wings are unique to these lintels. (Phimai Museum)

Found to the east of the main prang, this lintel shows Indra standing on the heads of the elephant Airavata and preparing to hurl his thunderbolt. It has many features which may be compared with a lintel from Prasat Damrei No 269 in Cambodia. In both representations, Indra is shown standing on the heads of Airavata and the costumes and decorations are in the Koh Ker style with the sampots tucked in a curved line under the stomach. The top row of the Damrei lintel carries praying deities, while here the top row consists of cross-legged rishis. Also the garland and foliage are stiffer and flatter. In addition the ends of the garland have here been carved in the form of Gana riding on his own trunk, an iconographical detail not popular in contemporary Khmer carving but used during the earlier Bakheng period (c.893-925 AD) and the later Pre Rup style (947-965 AD). Thus the dating can be interpreted in two ways - either the carver was copying an older style or he was in the forefront of a new one. (Phimai Museum)

This unfinished lintel has recently been discovered. Although only the basic outlines have been carved, it is possible to deduce from the placement of the elements and the decorative line that it forms part of the same group of lintels. Two interpretations of the story depicted are possible. Firstly, that the lintel depicts the story of Krishnavatara when Krishna kills Kamsa. Comparable scenes which definitedly depict this incident are the lintel from inside the southern entrance of the mandapa of Wat Phu in Laos and the inner lintel of the western prang porch of Phnom Rung. However, as the face of the main actor has not been fully carved this attribution cannot be confirmed. A second interpretation based on the square shape of his face, his right cheek left bare for the carving of a fang, and a seemingly hairy chest, suggests the story of Narasimhavatara (a man-lion), in which Vishnu is transformed into a Narasimha and kills Hiranya. If the lintel illustrates the Krishnavatara, then Krishna should be shown as a young man with his hair pulled up on his head, whereas here his hair is loose and flowing at the back. These characteristics are not typical of Vishnu as Krishna but rather as a Narasimha.

Unusually Prasat Muang Khaek does not face east and this northern gopura was the main entrance. The significance of this has not yet become apparent. Even though the base is all that remains, it is possible to appreciate its scale and importance.

Seen from the north-west, the sandstone bases of the outer walls lead to the large northern gopura. Above this sandstone base would have been a brick wall, enclosing the entire area of the prasat; its original height is unknown. Between the outer and inner walls is a moat. The door frames of the main prang are just visible in the distance.

To the east of the main prang is a long chamber which may have been developed in later periods as a gallery. The construction of such long rooms roofed with wood and tiles began in the Bakheng period (c.893-925AD). Those that can be studied, apart from here, exist at Prasat Thom, although there the long chamber differs in having a wall on one side and a row off columns on the other. Here, both sides were closed of by brick walls, and in the distance can be seen another wall closing off the chamber to the south, also of brick. In the foreground is the entrance door, while roughly halfway along the chamber is an entrance to the courtyard of the prasat. The eastern wall (on the left) would seem to have had rectangular window openings. All in all this long chamber is significantly different from contemporary styles in Cambodia.

SI KHIU STONE QUARRY

แหล่งตัดหินสีคิ้ว

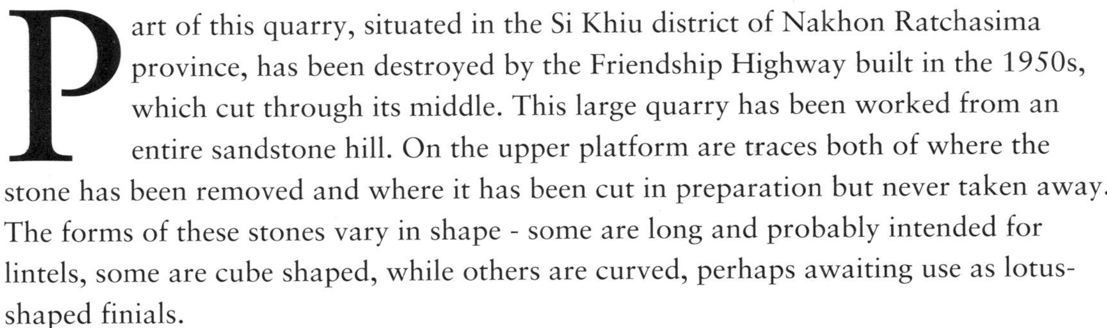

Part of this quarry, situated in the Si Khiu district of Nakhon Ratchasima province, has been destroyed by the Friendship Highway built in the 1950s, which cut through its middle. This large quarry has been worked from an entire sandstone hill. On the upper platform are traces both of where the stone has been removed and where it has been cut in preparation but never taken away. The forms of these stones vary in shape - some are long and probably intended for lintels, some are cube shaped, while others are curved, perhaps awaiting use as lotus-shaped finials.

To the south of this sandstone hill there is a large open area from where all the stone has been removed and today villagers use it for tapioca planting. We do not know where the stone was actually used, and no scientific tests have been carried out, but it lies only a few kilometres directly to the east from Prasat Non Ku and Muang Khaek.

BAN KRUAT STONE QUARRIES

แหล่งตัดหินบ้านกรวด

Situated in the Ban Kruat district of Buriram province is an area covering over one square kilometre, in which piles of sandstone blocks are scattered over many small hillocks. This is where Khmer stonecarvers came for the stone with which to build numerous temples. The quarries are only 20 kilometres from Phnom Rung as the crow flies; nevertheless scientific tests have not been used to establish whether stone from this quarry was actually used at that site.

Ban Kruat differs from the Si Khiu quarry in that the stone from here is widely scattered across the site and is not grouped in the form of a large hill as at Si Khiu.

Of particular interest here is that over such a wide area it is possible to see all the stages involved in quarrying the blocks of stone. Light incisions mark the outline of what would be cut into a vertical trench a few centimetres wide. Intersecting trenches mark out rectangular blocks which would later be cut through at the base. Closely spaced vertical holes were a method of effecting deep vertical breaks.

PRASAT PHNOM WAN

ปราสาทพนมวัน

Opposite
The plan of the prasat is consistent with those built on flat plains dating from the 11th to the beginning of the 12th century. It is made up of a main prang which has porches on all four sides, with an antarala joined to the mandapa. This type of plan occurs both at Phimai and Phnom Rung, but this site differs from them in that its antarala is longer and the walls are pierced by windows on both sides. In contrast, Phimai's has a false window on each side and Phnom Rung has an entrance on each side. The similarity between Phnom Rung and Phnom Wan is that the antarala is placed at the centre of the site. If one were to draw a line from the east gopura to the west gopura and from the north gopura to the south gopura, these two lines would bisect each other exactly at the antarala. This feature is unusual in that such a bisection would normally occur at the main prang, such as at Phimai. There must, therefore, be some additional significance to the design which remains hidden from us. Although the prasat is built on a flat plain, the base is neither high nor complicated compared with a site such as Phimai. Nevertheless, the base is higher than at Phnom Rung, presumably because the latter was already built on a mountain top.

Stone hand of Uma holding a lotus. (Mahavirawong Museum, Khorat)

Stone linga.

Situated between the modern city of Khorat and the ancient site of Phimai. Phnom Wan was catalogued by both Aymonier and de Lajonquière. Three important inscriptions dated 891, 1055 and 1082 AD have been found at the site. The last of these, inscribed on the doorjamb of the southern porch, mentions the monastery at Phimai. While the fifty or so kilometres between the two temples can be covered today in under an hour, in the 11th century the distance was a substantial undertaking. In addition, there are many other contemporary temples in the Phnom Wan region such as Non Ku and Muang Khaek. Thus the mention of Phimai, known to be an important city at this time, makes the establishment of particular interest. This link, and the fine and early carving at Phnom Wan testify to a venerable monastic establishment.

Little remains today of the wide moat which once enclosed the temple. To the east is a large baray or reservoir, about half a kilometre in length. Remains of a further reservoir, over a kilometre in length, are visible on aerial photographs of the area. All these bodies of waters completed a microcosmic recreation of the Hindu universe. The central Mount Meru, home of the gods, was surrounded by a wall. Beyond the wall lay the sacred oceans. Fulfillment of this plan ensured harmony with the gods, bringing prosperity to the kingdom. At Phnom Wan, the wall is represented by the gallery which forms a rectangle around the central sanctuary. The plan is similar to Phimai, except that the two side gopuras, which at Phimai are offset to align with the doorways of the central cell, are centered in the side galleries of Phnom Wan.

The earliest evidence for the temple's existence underlies the east-facing annex found in the southern sector of the courtyard. Although this building is today a jumble of sanstone blocks and bricks, the base is made up of the very large bricks typical of 7-9th century remains. As at Phnom Rung, it may be that a second or third brick tower once existed which was covered over during construction of the sandstone sanctuary seen today. Clearly the temple was altered and added to over several centuries, from at least the late 9th century through the end of the 11th century. Parts of the corbelled roof, all sandstone blocks, still remains intact. Altogether, the temple measures more than 25 metres in length. Although the building is predominantly built of white sandstone, parts of the roof are red sandstone and the red stone has also been used to make the rounded bobbin columns in the windows.

An inscription bearing the date 891 AD, written in Sanskrit, was found on one of the doorjambs at Phnom Wan. It refers to two early kings who reigned at Angkor, Indravarman I (867-889 AD) and Yasovarman I (889-910 AD). A lintel from Phnom Wan, now at the Bangkok National Museum, provides further evidence for Phnom Wan's existence by at least the second half of the 9th century (late Preah Ko style). A kala occupies the centre of the lintel, his face and head composed of wonderfully expressive curls of foliage. A garland issues from his mouth, and from the garland emerges two triple-headed nagas. The creatures are arched upwards, with further vegetative swirls rising up to crown their heads. The rest of the lintel continues this motif, the curls taking on the form of soft wings on the upper register. Both the looseness of the curls and the depth of the carving make this piece unique.

A contrast in styles, and proof of continued work on the temple some two hundred years later, is offered by the in situ lintel over the north entrance of the sanctuary.

Another lintel, dated to the end of the Bakheng period (first half of the 10th century), shows that the popularity of the kala motif did not inhibit other scenes. In this case, the central figure is the god Vishnu, mounted atop a rather sturdy rendition of his vehicle Garuda who, as is often shown, demonstrates his mastery over his arch enemy, the subterranean naga. The tails of the two nagas are grasped firmly in the Garuda's hands. The bodies of the nagas curve upward and then across the length of the lintel. Various devatas dance on the back of the nagas, some unusually depicted with a lion-like body and a tail.

As so much of the temple is no longer intact, it is difficult to tell to which deity it was principally dedicated. Certainly during some of its existence, however, the Hindu god Shiva was pre-eminent. The 1055 AD inscription on the southern doorjamb mentions a Saivite monastery. Two other traces of Shiva worship are a carved stone hand holding a lotus, identified as Shiva's consort Uma, and a large stone linga, both now in the Mahavirawong Museum in Nakhon Ratchasima.

Finds of Buddha images suggest that the temple was used well into the 12th and 13th centuries when Buddhist worship became the norm. This custom continues today - images of the Buddha from many different periods fill the dimly lit interior of the temple, which is still used for worship. Much remains to be learned about the Phnom Wan complex, and its relationship to Phimai.

Stone head of a Buddha protected by naga. (Mahavirawong Museum, Khorat)

Buddha under naga, 13th century. This image together with the head fragment below left, show the local workman attempting to copy bronze Buddha images. (Mahavirawong Museum, Khorat)

Opposite
Buddha torso, 13th century, with replaced cement head and hands. Phnom Wan was converted to Buddhism in the 13th century as evidenced by various Buddha images. Sadly all, like this one, have been beheaded by vandals and all the hands and heads have been replaced by the local people.

Stone statue of a female deity, late Baphuon style, end of the 11th century. This statue has been discovered in recent excavations to the west of the small prang. There is some slight damage to the figure - her right breast is chipped and the feet broken off - but the rest is in reasonably good condition. Her hand positions, with the right turned down, the left turned up, suggest that the figure might represent Uma, whose right hand is normally shown holding the staff of a club while her left hand holds a dharni (an orb representing the earth). (Mahavirawong Museum, Khorat)

Opposite
The rough dressing of the sandstone blocks used to construct the southern gopura is highlighted by the early morning sun. The main prang lies beyond.

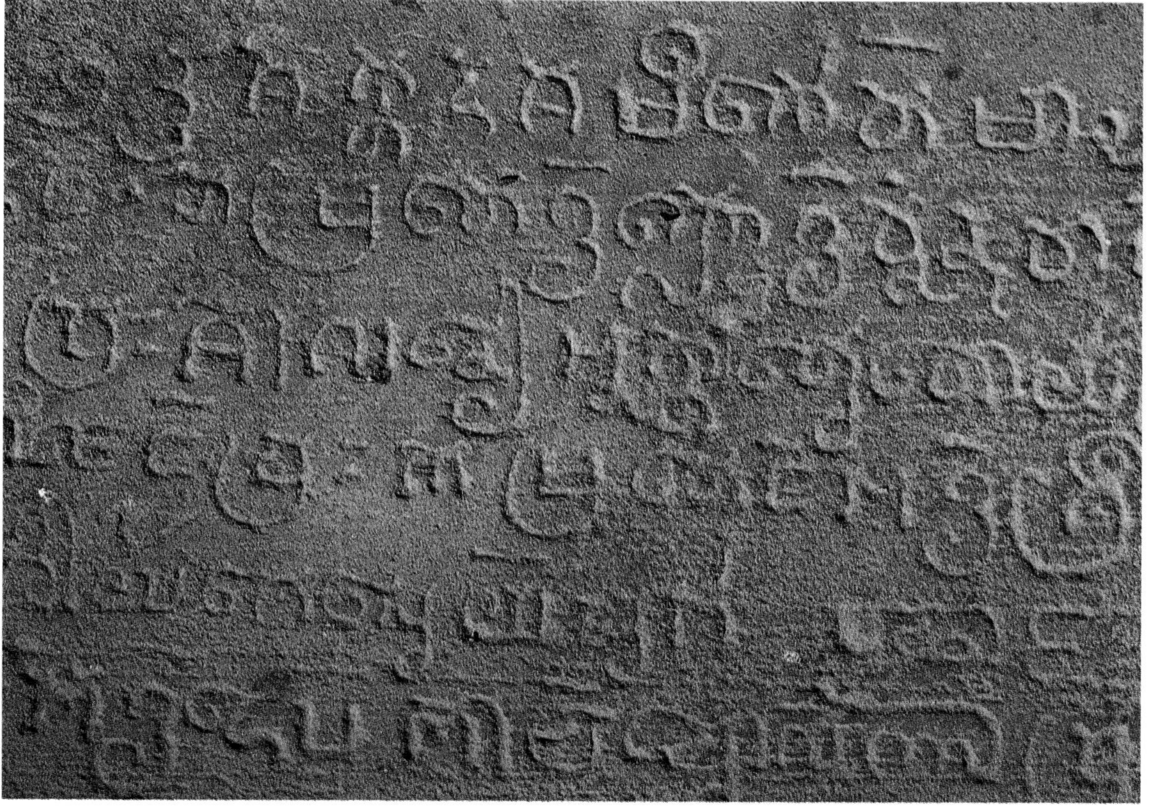

Inscription on the inner frame of the door. Several inscriptions have been found at this site, generally on the doorjambs. In the main prang, two inscriptions date to 1055 and 1082 AD in the reigns of King Udayadityavarman II and Jayavarman VI. From these we learn that this building was dedicated to Shiva; in addition there was probably a dwelling for a rishi, as the inscription of King Jayavarman VI refers to one.

The remains of the smaller prang in the southwest corner of the enclosure. The lack of carving makes dating imprecise but the plan suggests an 11th century date contemporary with the main prang.

Overleaf
Inside the mandapa chamber adorned with various Buddha statues.

แม่แดง-ด.ช.ป่าน
ด.ญ.ปุ้ย จิตรสุวรรณ

Lintel showing Vishnu riding Garuda, Bakheng style, early 10th century. All the elements in the lintel, from the nagas held by Garuda to the costumes of the various figures and the coiled foliage below, leave one in little doubt that the lintel dates from the Bakheng period (c.893-925 AD). However these elements are different from those found in Cambodia, in that they are stiffer and somewhat lifeless. The Garuda may be compared with the one from Prasat Kravan at Angkor in the Bakheng period. Nevertheless, the dancing deities are full of movement and make one think of those from the Koh Ker period. Thus this lintel could date from the late Bakheng period when the style was beginning to change to that of Koh Ker, in the first half of the 10th century. (Phimai Museum, Khorat)

Lintel in the Baphuon style, 11th century. This lintel shows the typical features of the style such as the kalas spewing forth garlands on both sides. The most important feature is the divinity sitting atop the kala flanked by two sword-bearing attendants. However, the divinity's lack of attributes prevents his identification. (Phimai Museum, Khorat)

This recently discovered lintel depicting kala face disgorging garlands is the most beautiful Preah Ko lintel found in Thailand. The kala face can be compared to those on the lintel at Prasat Kok Po in Cambodia. Round flower motifs at the centre of each half and the water lilies at various parts of the lintel point to the Preah Ko style. Naga heads at the extremities of the garlands seem to make their first appearance in this style (National Museum, Bangkok). Photo: Mark Williams

The lintel from the north porch of the main prang, in the Baphuon style, dates to the 11th century. Here, the kala has his customary arms, absent in the earlier lintels. The garland of foliage issuing from the kala's mouth is still deeply carved, but is considerably thinner than before. Finally, the foliate swirls are now elongated and tighter. The total effect achieved is one of great verticality, whereas the elements of the 9th century Preah Ko lintels seem to slide gently sideways.

As at Phimai, a distinctive red sandstone makes an occasional, decorative appearance. Here, the baluster of a partially collapsed window makes a contrast in colour with its supporting frame.

The foliage decorating the pilaster of the main prang illustrates the 11th century style by the manner in which the lotus stem has been incised with two vertical lines.

Overleaf
Phnom Wan taken from the north-west corner showing the main sanctuary with its antarala and mandapa.

PREAH VIHEAR (KHAO PHRA VIHARN)

ปราสาทเขาพระวิหาร

Opposite
The fifth gopura. This is the first gopura that one encounters when climbing up the steps to the prasat from the Thai side and, moreover, it is the finest gopura in an architectural sense - cruciform in plan with a porch, pediment and doorway on all four sides and, originally, a wooden-framed tile roof. Columns along the length of the gopura give it an unusually light and airy feeling. The two bottom corners of the upper pediment curve outwards and while this form evolved from the portrayal of two makaras, it is here more creative and inventive. This style of pediment seems to have begun to be used during the Koh Ker period (compare Prasat Krachap in Cambodia) and was further developed at Banteay Srei, before appearing here at Preah Vihear.

A boundary post on the causeway between Gopuras IV and V is one of 65 on each side, in the shape of a lotus bud.

This magnificent temple built and added to over many reigns occupies the most spectacular site of any Khmer sanctuary. The cause of a border dispute between Cambodia and Thailand settled eventually in Cambodia's favour, the temple was designed to be approached from the north, now on the Thai side of the border. Known as Preah Vihear in Khmer, it is called Khao Phra Viharn by the Thais.

For the Khmer, a sanctuary was above all a cosmological recreation. A mountain or cliff top location would be the first choice for Khmer architects building a major temple. This is especially true in temples dedicated to Shiva because of the associations with his mountain home, Mount Kailasa. The other signficant mountain top temple in Thailand is Phnom Rung. The tower at the centre of the complex symbolized Mount Meru, the mountain home of the gods. Its floorplan was small, being only a fraction of the sacred enclosure. The rings of mountains and seas which surround the mount were represented in the Khmer temple by walls and moats, which were arranged about the central shrine, either concentrically, or, as was the case at Preah Vihear, in a lengthwise plan. The horizontal spread of subsidiary buildings complemented the verticality of the temple tower. The result was a low but vast expanse, either open to the sky or pierced with windows to lighten dark stone corridors. Only the tower housing the shrine to the gods was sheltered from the light.

The elements of the Hindu shrine - walls, moats, towers - were used by the Khmer in two different ways. At Angkor, they were combined into temple mountains, sanctuaries built by one king, personifying his sole right to rule. However, at Angkor, and throughout Northeast Thailand, sanctuaries were added to over hundreds of years. Many places may have previously been associated with local nature and ancestral spirits, and the erection of a Hindu stone structure paid homage to these deities as well as the new gods. This amalgamation of beliefs helps to explain the adherence of the ordinary Khmer to the undertakings of their rulers, a loyalty which demanded much labour. In the process, pre-existing deities were transformed into Hindu gods, most often Shiva, with their ancestral abode becoming the temple. Hinduism in India was a syncretic religion, but in the world of the Khmer, the pantheon of manifested and implied spirits grew even larger.

Location & Approach

The temple is aligned from north to south on a rocky south-facing spur of the Dangrek Range which forms the Thai-Cambodian border. The sanctuary walls reach almost to the edge of the escarpment, a height of nearly 600 metres, which then forms a sheer drop 500 metres down, to the Cambodian plain. On the Thai side, forest covers the lower hills. Where the trees thin out, the temple begins. The staircases, gopuras, processional walkways and courtyards stretch about 850 metres along the length of the outcrop, rising some 120 metres in height from entry to summit. The first 80 metres of the approach are staircases, wide at first, and then narrowing as they become steeper. Some of the steps have been carved from the rocky outcrop, the rest having been brought from nearby quarries.

The first pause comes at a 30-metre long platform bordered by a naga balustrade. The bodies of the serpent, about a metre thick, are carved from sandstone blocks. Their multiple heads rear up at the ends, facing north down the staircase. The style of the nagas' heads, smooth, without crowns, is very similar to that seen at Prasat Muang Tam, suggesting an 11th century date for this part of the temple.

After the naga balustrade, the first of the cruciform gopuras is reached. As the outermost of the five gateways, it is known as Gopura V. Although much of it has fallen down, some of the door structures remain. All are finely carved, particularly the pediments with their poly-lobed frames in the shape of the body of the naga bordered by a flame-like foliage. A pathway going east from this gopura leads down towards a stream, said to have once been a reservoir. The main entryway to the temple, however, continues towards the south. A causeway, 270 metres long and 11 metres wide, is lined with lotus-shaped pillars, similar to those found at Prasat Phnom Rung. Remains of a smaller rectangular pond are found to the east of the causeway. Gopura IV at the end of the avenue is set on a foundation, similar to Gopura V, although the cruciform plan has been extended on both axes. The tiered pediments are typical of this period of Khmer architecture and may be compared with those found at Banteay Srei. This gopura is more complete than the outermost one, and the style of the carvings and the presence of three 11th century inscriptions date it to the late Khleang and early Baphuon periods. Motifs on the lintels and pediments include the ever-present kala or kirtimukha head, popular also at the 11th century temple of Muang Tam. Nagas are featured in a number of guises: there are finely carved scenes of Krishna killing the serpent Kaliya, Vishnu reclining on the serpent Sesha, and above this on the pediment facing south towards the temple, the story of the Churning of the Sea of Milk, the body of the serpent wrapped around Mount Mandara to extract the elixir of immortality from the primordial ocean.

A second causeway continues south from Gopura IV. It, too, would have once been lined with boundary pillars. A small stone-lined pool to the east is called the 'lion-head' pool, after the head of a lion built into its southern side. At the end of the causeway, some 152 metres in length, is the third, or outermost courtyard (as with the

The massive nagas on either side of the 'naga bridge' are in the true Baphuon style, their heads bare of all decoration and their necks held high unlike the fat and podgy nagas of earlier styles such as at the Bakong. It is only later that such naga balustrades were raised above the ground on supports as at Phnom Rung.

The tip of the pediment frame of Gopura V is finely carved with a dancing deity.

gopuras, the first courtyard is the one closest to the temple). The east and west courtyards which flank Gopura III take this axis of the temple complex to its widest point before narrowing again in the second and first courtyards. The final causeway between the third and second courtyards has shortened also, to about 36 metres in length. Remains of a naga balustrade flank the boundary pillars on the outside.

The second courtyard is formed by Gopura II and I to the north and south respectively, while a gallery and short wall close off the sides. To the south of this courtyard, the remains of a large antechamber lead into the doorway of Gopura I. Two 'libraries' flank this hall on either side.

The final gopura of the temple, Gopura I leads into a courtyard containing the mandapa and the totally collapsed prang behind. Intact galleries, lined with windows on the courtyard side, form the walls to the east and west. The south side is formed by a blind gopura abutting the very edge of the cliff. Doors in the outer walls give access to annex buildings to the east and west, possibly used for royal rituals or preparation for ceremonial dances.

It is not known when construction first began at Preah Vihear. Most of the existing structures, notably much of the third courtyard where inscriptions from this period are found, date only to the reign of Suryavarman I. Indeed it is believed that this site was his personal temple and that the main prang used to house a Bhadresvara or linga which was used in ceremonies to release the sacred power from the Lingaparvata at Wat Phu near Champasak, 130 kilometeres to the east. Equally, the carving of the main sanctuary and the naga balustrades and the boundary posts also date to this era. Further inscriptions were erected at Preah Vihear under Suryavarman II (1113-1150) and his chief priest, Divakarapandita. Suryavarman II is also thought to have finished or altered parts of the second courtyard, the causeways, and the staircases. After this time, the temple appears to have fallen into disrepair.

The ruins of the temple today guard many secrets about its use from the 9th to 12th century. The graceful forms carved from stone depict not only the gods, but animals, both mythical and real, and the rich foliage of the forest. The inscriptions, in praising the gods, evoke other images. Ritual feasts and offerings included peacock feather fans with gold handles, rings with nine jewels, and golden bowls. The life of the court was filled with colour and music, for the temple also required offerings of dancers, flower receptacles, sacred cloths, incense and candles.

This interior of Gopura IV showing the square holes carved into the backs of the pediments and in which the wooden purlins were inserted.

Gopura IV is cruciform in plan and like Gopura V would have had a wood frame tiled roof. The southern wall seen here is solid, while the northern face of the building is composed of a row of four-sided pillars.

The pediment from the southern doorway of Gopura IV is one of the finest yet discovered. It illustrates a story which was extremely popular in Khmer iconography, namely the Churning of the Sea of Milk. Mount Mandara can be seen being used as a pivot in the middle with Brahma seated above in an unusual position. Vishnu has entwined himself around the pole-shaped mountain, to command the gods and demons to turn the pivot. The stirring of the ocean in this carving is shown as taking place inside a pot. The gods are on the left at the tail end of the Naga Vasuki, whilst the demons are at his head. In this representation, however, the gods and the demons are so alike that it is almost impossible to distinguish between them. On either side of Brahma can be seen the sun and the moon, below which are the rishis. On the extreme left can be seen a seated thin man who is merely skin and bones. This is Bringin, Shiva's disciple. Next to him is the Garuda who is constantly trying to steal the elixir of eternal life. On one side of the pot containing the elixir can be seen the head of Ucchaisaravas, while Lakshmi is seated on the other. On the far right of the scene is a figure on an elephant and this is Indra. Above Indra is a rishi and nearby a flying figure representing Dhanwantari who is normally shown emerging from the pot holding the elixir. In the story, the elixir is in turn stolen from him by the demons and while they are debating who will take the first sip, Vishnu transformed into Mohini distracts them with her dancing and takes back the pot. Here we are only shown the story up to the point at which Dhanwantari appears with the elixir. At the base of the lintel Vishnu has transformed into a turtle to support Mount Mandara and prevent it sinking into the ground.

Pillar capital. An interesting feature of Gopura V is the traces of red paint that still remain, which microscopic examination has confirmed as haematite (an iron ore). This could either have been applied as a background colour or as a base to receive gold leaf. There is evidence that important religous sites were sometimes covered with bronze or gold. Red paint was generally used as a base coat before the application of gold leaf.

Umamahesvara on the southern inner pediment of the Gopura III. This representation of Umamahesvara illustrates that the sculptors had not yet come to abhor uncarved space behind the image. This style was characteristic of the early 11th century. Uma and Shiva are riding on the bull Nandin through a forest, represented by a single tree, and are surrounded by their various followers.

The middle door from the southern facade of Gopura III seen from Gopura II. This gopura is the largest at Preah Vihear and the construction of its roof differs from the others, having had wooden beams with bricks rather than the usual terracotta tiles.

The western doorway of the south side of Gopura III. The pediment shows a deity sitting cross-legged above a kala.

The back of the west 'library', one of two in the second courtyard. The false porch and its tiered pediments project only slightly from the main structure.
Both 'libraries' are built from sandstone with the exception of the roof which would have been tiled with brick. The use of many convex and concave curves on the pediments was a style that began to develop at Banteay Srei. The sides of the 'library' carry half-pediments with roofs, giving the impression that the building is divided into a nave and two side aisles, a type of construction known as a 'false triple nave' - in reality, the inside plan is one simple rectangle.The nagas at the corners of the pediments have foliate head-dresses of the late 10th century, while the lintel is in typical 11th century style. Overall its appearance places this building in the Khleang-Baphuon style.

Opposite
The eastern 'library' facing inwards towards the second courtyard, seen from the roof of Gopura I. It is rectangular with a small protruding porch at the front, allowing access, while the rear facade has a false door together with a pediment and a lintel. The 'library' is lit solely by rectangular horizonatal windows piercing the upper part of the walls above the side-roofs.

Overleaf
The mandapa and collapsed main prang seen from the north-west corner of the surrounding gallery.

False doors, fully decorated, are set into both sides of the southern wall. Left, the door at the south-west corner, facing out over the plains below, has strongly curved motifs in its pediment and lintel. The frame of the pediment is decorated with a floral branch in which the flowers point down, a style of foliage popular at the beginning of the 11th century. The nagas at the ends of the pediment have beautifully

carved floral head-dresses. In the middle of the pediment is a deity riding on a kala in the midst of a foliated garland, a type of decoration which is found on other architectural elements during the Baphuon period such as pilasters, colonettes and door panels of both real and false doors. Right, a naga antefix decorates the tiered pediment above and marks the outer corner of the enclosure.

Opposite
The southeast corner of the galleries surrounding the main prang is built right up to the edge of the 500 metre cliff overhang and decorated with a false door.

This carving which has recently been discovered in a cliff (near the viewing platform) to the north of the temple at Mo Ee Daeng, shows an unidentified deity sitting with his right elbow resting on his right knee with two goddesses seated on either side. The flower tucked behind his ear, is normally associated with demon giants (cf Jean Boisselier), and it is possible that this carving may represent Kubera, the leader of the giants.

A pair of stone shrines with coved roofs were found at Mo Ee Daeng, north of the main complex. These differ in form from any Khmer buildings previously encountered, and have no entrance. After thieves broke in and looted the shrines, we can now deduce from the remaining bases that originally each shrine contained a statue. Today, we are no closer to solving the mystery of these unusual buildings.

TA MUEN THOM

ปราสาทตาเมือนธม

Opposite
This north-western sandstone prang is one of a pair flanking the central structure and is the most complete in the sanctuary. Perhaps its condition may be explained by the fact that no carving had been done on the prang and so it was of no interest to the looters. When de Lajonquière visited the site he reported that it and its pair were in good condition. However it is strange that he noted brick as the construction material. In fact, only the upper part of the inner walls are of brick; laterite is used below, while the large uncarved sandstone blocks of the outer walls recall Ta Keo at Angkor. Another significant feature is that the three false doors are carved from single blocks of stone, a characteristic which has not been found anywhere else in Thailand.

Situated in Kab Choeng district, Surin province are the remains of Ta Muen Thom built in the 11th century. The Dangrek Range divides the lower part of Northeast Thailand's Khorat Plateau from Cambodia. Along much of the Dangreks the escarpment of the plateau towers over the Cambodian plain below. Temples such as Preah Vihear, which overlook this precipice, can only easily be approached from the Thai side of the border. However, at a few places, passes exist through the mountain range. Given the topography, temples which commanded these passes were of great strategic value. The sanctuary at Ta Muen Thom is one of these temples on the road connecting Angkor with Phimai and for centuries was one of the finest stone temples of this period. Sadly, the destruction seen at the site today does not date to the period of the temple's occupancy, but to recent history.

Khmer Rouge troops occupied the temple, and in the course of several skirmishes wreaked severe damage to the structure. In the ensuing years, treasure seekers almost completed the task, chiselling off every potentially saleable bas-relief from the temple façade. Reconstruction has begun, but the task is more difficult than usual. Recent excavations have uncovered many interesting discoveries such as several inscriptions yet to be deciphered and a svayambhu (a natural rock linga) on a pedestal hewn directly from the bedrock. This clearly determined the site, as it is enclosed by the garbhagrha. The main tower was built on a natural rock platform that extends as far as the east and west gopuras, and has been carved with a number of holes and insets. A somasutra follows a natural channel in the bedrock that leads out from the garbhagrha. The latter indicates the relative importance of this site.

A massive laterite staircase leads down from the southern gopura into Cambodia, and some 20 metres beyond this is a platform at the edge of a stream. A landing platform constructed near the stream is at the foot of a monumental staircase leading up the hill, a distance of some 30 metres. The surrounding gallery of the temple has four gopuras, with the principal entry being on the south. Inside the gallery, the central sanctuary and two additional prangs to the north are built of a pinky-grey sandstone. Two intact laterite buildings are also found in the courtyard, one of a rectangular plan near the eastern wall and another square cell located by the western wall, as well as the foundations of other buildings.

A silk cotton tree towers over the western gallery at sunset.

Part of the northern gopura. Strangler fig (Ficus religiosa) and silk cotton trees (Ceiba pentandra) throughout the site have become intertwined among the blocks of laterite and sandstone. Such vegetation is reminiscent of Ta Prohm and Preah Khan at Angkor.

Overleaf
In the north-eastern corner of the enclosure the rubble of sandstone blocks is not the decay of an abandoned temple but the work of thieves seeking artefacts.

The scale of destruction can be appreciated by comparing the sepia photographs taken 20 years ago with all that remains today. Photo : Smitthi Siribhadra
Left: *the head of a guardian from the central prang has been crudely removed.*

Right and above: *the north side of the temple. Above may be seen a capital and the naga end of the pediment shown in full at right. This pediment and lintel are from the end of the 11th century in the late Baphuon style. A similar lintel style may be seen in Phnom Wan, Muang Tam and Preah Vihear.*

The savayambhu, or natural linga, in the shrine of the central sanctuary, resting on a stepped circular pedestal that has been hewn out of the underlying rock. This recent discovery (the first excavation took place in 1992) confirms that Ta Muen Thom had a special importance.

A natural fissure in the bed-rock leads out from the shrine towards the north-east gallery wall in the foreground. The builders took advantage of this to construct an unusually long somasutra for draining the lustral waters poured over the linga.

Overleaf
The now-cleared enclosure of the temple, looking south form the north-west corner. The shrine, antarala and mandapa on the left are built partly on the sandstone foundation of the escarpment. The trees beyond mark the national frontier and the descent to the Cambodian plain.

PRASAT KAMPHAENG YAI

ปราสาทกำแพงใหญ่

Opposite
The restored main prang with its projecting porch facing east (at the right of the picture) and the finely carved southern pediment depicting Umamahesvara. The top of the prang has collapsed and it is no longer possible to ascertain from what material, or materials, this would have been constructed. The two side prangs, together with the single prang to the south-west, are built of brick except for the sandstone door frames, columns and lintels. Before excavation by the Fine Arts Department these prangs were almost half buried in earth.

Below
The porch of the central prang before excavation.

The Mun River becomes broader as it flows east across the Khorat Plateau.There are fewer tributaries and over the centuries the river has cut more deeply into the flat alluvium. During the rainy season, waterways in the eastern province of Sisaket easily overflow their banks. During the extended dry season from November to March, there is little or no precipitation. Economically this region is one of Thailand's poorest.

It is also the home of one of the most spectacular Khmer objects found in recent years. During excavations by the Fine Arts Department at Prasat Kamphaeng Yai in Uthumphon Phisai district, a large bronze guardian figure was unearthed in the inner courtyard. The discovery was only 10 centimeters underground, near the southwestern gate. Portions of lifesize bronzes have been found, such as the torso of a reclining figure of Vishnu found at Angkor and a bronze head from Ban Tanot in Northeast Thailand. The only known full-figure bronzes are not nearly as fine, and as a result of various wars have been moved from Cambodia to Ayutthaya to Burma (Myanmar), and today are kept in Mandalay. Thus the provenance as well as fineness of execution, make the guardian from Kamphaeng Yai quite unique.

The Temple plan

Although the bronze guardian is the most recent and spectacular result of the Fine Arts Department's excavations, many instances of fine carving and the plan of the temple suggest that it was a prosperous establishment.

The temple complex is found behind a modern wat outside the town of Ban Kamphaeng Yai. The wall of the temple's name (Kamphaeng Yai meaning 'large wall' in Thai) is an imposing sandstone and laterite gallery, over fifty metres on each side, with a gopura at each of the four cardinal points. The main, eastern, gopura has three doorways to the courtyard and is in the form of a cross. Just before entering the courtyard, there is an inscription in Khmer carved on the left side. Still intact are the horizontal windows of the gallery walls. Similar windows are seen in the 'libraries' of Preah Vihear and Phnom Rung, and may date to the early 11th century.

From the carving of the lintels, it would seem that the buildings were constructed at different times. Thus the lintel from the central tower combines stylistic elements from the

10th century Banteay Srei period and the later Khleang style of Angkor Thom, whereas the lintel from the north 'library', depicting a reclining Vishnu, is in the 11th century Baphuon style. In addition lion guardians at the base of the central tower are typical of that period.

The sanctuary was probably dedicated to Shiva as evidenced by an inscription in which Kamrateng Añ Shivatasa gave the land for the glory of Bridheshvara which would seem to refer to Shiva. The site consists of six extant buildings. All are of brick except for the central prang which is a mixed construction of sandstone and brick with a brick superstructure. At the centre of the enclosure is the main prang, flanked north and south by two small prangs. Behind the southern prang stands another, and, given the Khmer love of symmetry, it is likely that its pair was planned but never built. In the east of the enclosure are two brick annexes facing west in the position usually occupied by 'libraries'.

An image of the Buddha seated on a naga measuring over a metre high was formerly housed in the modern vihara which adjoined the main temple. It was found at the base of the main tower. This image has now been moved to the new monastery constructed outside the ancient site.

Opposite
The rear of the northern prang (foreground) and main prang (beyond), after excavation but before restoration. Before the excavation was completed by the Fine Arts Department, the level of the earth reached the top of the high base; some of it can be seen still adhering to the stone and brickwork.

Pilaster detail from the central prang. During the 11th century animals were used to decorate the lower parts of pilasters and were shown either spewing forth or holding the foliage.

The central row of three prangs, following excavation but before restoration (left), following restoration (right). The main prang, together with the northern and southern prangs, are nominally constructed on the same base, but while the central part, supporting the main prang, is sandstone, the two outer adjoining portions are of laterite.

Only the central prang at this site has a protruding porch on the front facade, and it comprises pilasters, a pediment and a lintel. The front walls of the porch and the cornice are of sandstone construction while the side walls are partly of brick.

Bronze guardian statue found at Kamphaeng Yai, Baphuon style, 11th century. This large bronze statue, some 126 cm in height excluding the base, is one of the finest surviving pieces of Khmer art and one of the most outstanding finds in recent years. The sombre-faced standing youth steps forward with his right leg, while his left hand rests on his hip. His right hand has been broken but was probably hanging down beside his body and holding a weapon. The statue's posture is reminiscent of the various Khmer guardian figures which date from the Preah Ko period onwards and in which generally a weapon would be held along the length of their bodies, while their other hand would rest on their hip. As this statue has been modelled in human form it would seem to be Nandikesvara who would normally be paired with a Mahakala in demon form. Nandikesvara would be on the right side of the prasat (our left), while Mahakala would be on the left of the prasat (or our right when entering the building).

The figure wears a short, pleated sampot with the edge turned in under his belly button with the two ends tied and sticking out. He wears a belt in the Baphuon style, decorated with panels incised with a double row of ovals and again small pendants hang off the belt at intervals. He wears a necklace decorated with floral motifs and beads or pearls, and at the back small pendants hang down.
The head and face of the figure are very interesting. On his head, the lines where his hair would probably have been pulled back into a jatamukuta are still visible, even thought the top part of the chignon has disappeared. His eyebrows, moustache, beard and mouth are deeply incised and they were probably inlaid with gold, reminiscent of the head of Shiva at Por Loboek, Siemreap and the large bronze of the reclining Vishnu found in the Western Baray at Angkor in the same period. Indeed, the whole figure was probably guilded in gold as many traces have been found on the statue. (National Museum, Bangkok)

Southern pediment from the central prang showing Umamahesvara, carved in the 11th century. Shiva is seated on the bull Nandin, while Uma is seated on his lap. Various attendants surround them. Nandin has been given very fine decorative apparel, while Shiva, Uma and the attendants are dressed in pure Baphuon style.

The inner lintel from the southern 'library' shows another representation of Umamahesvara. Although less well preserved, the bull has a very proud posture. Behind, squirrels and tree shrews climb and play among the branches.

The inner lintel from the northern 'library' showing Vishnu Anantasayin (reclining Vishnu). This lintel is of great interest for the study of Khmer art in Thailand, because although the theme is quite common in Khmer art, certain erotic characteristics shown here do not appear in similar representations in Cambodia. Both of Vishnu's wives, Lakshmi and Bhumidevi, are seated and are massaging his calves, while Vishnu has raised his left foot to touch the breast of Bhumidevi (see detail opposite). The naga heads in the top right hand corner have rudimentary crowns and are perhaps a prototype for those at Phnom Rung, which was previously thought to be the earliest appearance of the crowned naga.

Pilaster decoration from the south side of the central prang features whole four-petalled flowers within a diamond-shaped lozenge, interspersed with half sectioned four-petalled flowers. This particular pattern is more usually found in bands of horizontal decoration around bases, cornices, capitals, etc. and was to continue to be influential into the Ayutthaya period.

The interior lintel from the central prang features Indra riding Airavata above a kala, which in turn is flanked by two simhas spewing forth garlands.

The sanctuary that once was dedicated to Shiva and held his statue has long since fallen into decay, but the sacred nature of the site has continued long after. During the Bayon period the site was transformed into a Buddhist Mahayana temple (a Buddha image protected by naga was found here).

Indeed, Buddhism has proved the most enduring religion of this region and today a modern Theravada temple catches the rays of the setting sun and symbolizes the death of the old and the birth of the new, or the endless circle of birth and death.

PRASAT MUANG TAM

ปราสาทเมืองต่ำ

Opposite
The north-east pond and outer northern gopura at sunrise.

Right
Stone hand of Vishnu holding a discus, one of his four attributes. Both Vishnu and Shiva appear in the motifs at Muang Tam. This fragment of a statue was unearthed during excavations.

Prasat Muang Tam, the 'temple of the lower city', is only about eight kilometres from Prasat Phnom Rung in the Prakhon Chai district of Buriram province. On a sunny day, looking south to the Cambodian border from the temple on Phnom Rung hill, the immense baray of Muang Tam glitters on the floodplain below. Two hundred yards to the south in a secluded, wooded setting lies the temple complex itself. Little is known of its history as to date, no inscriptions have been found. Regional accounts state that Muang Tam was built after Prasat Phnom Rung, to serve as a residence for the governor. As the lintels of Muang Tam are stylistically a combination of the Khleang (c.965-c.1010) and Baphuon (c.1010-c.1080) styles, the complex must have been built after the first phase of building at Phnom Rung but before the later additions in the Angkor Wat style (c.1100-1175 AD). Although the main sanctuary was dedicated to Shiva, a small statue of Vishnu, fragments of which remain, has also been found. The presence of this figure in a Saivite temple was a common occurence.

A short walk from the road, the east gopura of the outer enclosure is the temple's principal entrance. Here, the face of one of the kala doorways, has been carved across two sandstone blocks (see page 170). Such breaks at critical junctures, common in Khmer decorative carving, offer a clue to the way in which the temple was built: masons first assembled the structure, followed by a team of artisans who began the delicate task of sculpting the stone. Their precision can be seen in the details of the foliage as it crosses from one block to another. Just inside the entrance a large (136 cm) and as-yet-unidentified stone statue was excavated during recent Fine Arts Department restorations.

Within the temple enclosure, four L-shaped ponds reflect the changing colours of the sky. The bodies of nagas surrounds the ponds, guarding their treasures. Remains of steps can be seen in the laterite blocks which line the pool. Ritual processions descended to the edge of the water, perhaps with a ceremonial conch, to gather the sacred waters in the service of the temple god.

A second eastern gopura allows entry into the inner enclosure. As in the outer gopura, each doorway is surmounted by a lintel and pediment carved with the rounded face of a kala. The creature's hands firmly grasp the garland issuing from its mouth, lips drawn back to reveal a fearsome set of teeth emphasized by the finely worked pattern of incisions around the mouth.

With the possible exception of the stately nagas which grace the cruciform terraces at the nearby Prasat Phnom Rung, nowhere in Khmer art is the mysterious power of the naga more eloquently depicted than at Muang Tam. The naga, like most popular Khmer motifs, changed over the centuries. Thus the five heads of the late 12th century nagas of Prasat Phnom Rung are crowned with a multi-tiered halo which forms a continuous lobed arc around their heads. In contrast, the Muang Tam many-headed nagas have the smooth heads characteristic of the late 11th century Baphuon style. The naga can be seen throughout the Muang Tam enclosure. He is first encountered above the outer gopura doorways, his sectioned body reared up in protection. A lotus, symbol of creation from the cosmic waters, is carved on his chest. Jewels can also be seen, sometimes singly, in other cases issuing forth in a stream from the naga's mouth. At the corners of the projecting porches, to the right and left as well, distinctive nagas rear up above the door frames, their bodies undulating down from the apex of the pediments. From their mouths issue garlands, which fall down in front of them.

In the central area of the compound are five brick prangs, four of them recently rebuilt. These probably symbolized the five-peaked Mount Meru, home of the gods. Thus, although a large linga has been excavated near the porch of the central prang and the prang can be interpreted as signifying Mount Kailasa, home of Shiva, it here would seem to have a double significance. Construction no doubt began in brick which was an easily-available material and then later sandstone would have been brought from the Dangrek Mountains to complete the buildings. Both the inner and outer enclosures are paved with laterite throughout - further evidence of the importance accorded to this site. The main prang which had collapsed has now been excavated at the front revealing various components such as the base, parts of a porch and its pediment, a lintel, door frames, and finely carved sandstone pilasters.

On the prasat in the northwest corner, is a lintel of the god Shiva, seated on his vehicle, the bull Nandin, with his consort Uma on his knee. Nandin stands on a pedestal, atop the face and hands of a kala. The kala grasps the leg of a rampant lion, from whose mouth issues the foliate garland.

The naga is not forgotten, but is seen on each half of the lintel, his body stretched horizontally along the upper portion. The naga on the right side has three heads, each separately crowned, whereas his companion on the left has five heads which appear to be sheltered by a common hood. Both nagas curve upward in the center of the lintel, bodies resting gently againt the floral arch sheltering Shiva and Uma. A row of small rishis or ascetics sit cross-legged in meditation along the top register.

The freedom accorded to the artisan carving the lintels can be appreciated when this row of rishis is compared to that on another lintel, this one resting on the ground of the courtyard at the time of this publication. This second lintel is similar to that of Shiva and Uma - a deity, perhaps Indra is seated atop the face of the kala. But here, the bodies of the nagas have been replaced by a row of pearls, and the elbows of the ascetics have been placed along the inner thigh, not perched on top of the knee as is the case on the

Shiva lintel. Other differences can be seen in the face of the kala, and details of the creatures jaw, eyes, tongue and hands. Whereas many of the elements of Khmer bas reliefs become quite standardized within different eras, the depiction of mythical animals such as the kala and naga seem to have inspired endless variations.

The work of the Fine Arts Department in removing the earth which has accumulated in the central courtyard has revealed many hitherto unknown aspects of the complex, in particular the plan of the monuments in the inner courtyard. Each of the four subsidiary brick prangs may have been built in honour of a different deity or ancestor. Whereas before excavation, the compound exuded a tranquil openness, now the close juxtaposition of the five brick prasats suggest a crowded ritual centre. In addition, two west-facing 'libraries' have been uncovered in the eastern sector of the inner courtyard.

The architectural construction and the lintels and colonettes date the temple to the 11th century Baphuon period, although some decorative features such as on the outer gopura lintels where the kala's sharp triangular tongue is extended and repetitive flowered triangles arching above his head show the influence of the previous Khleang period. Certain features of the complex such as the laterite enclosing wall may well date to a later period.

Another feature of Muang Tam which indicates long-term use of the site, with building taking place over several hundred years, are the two baray or reservoirs. Leaving the main entrance to the compound, one passes through the courtyard of a modern wat, fragrant with ancient frangipani trees. Beyond, is a small reservoir. It is unexcavated, and its relationship with the temple enclosure is unclear. However, as it is precisely aligned with the central door of the outer gopura, it may well have been part of the original plan.

A second, later, reservoir is seen immediately north of the temple compound. Its size far exceeds the earlier baray, measuring 1,150 x 400 metres. Rectangular baray can be found throughout the Northeast, their angularity distinguishing them from natural ponds. They range in size from small tanks for family use, to this massive baray and the even larger one, just north of Prasat Phnom Wan.

The significant aspect of the Muang Tam baray is the ingenious way that it has been sited to take advantage of the landscape. The land upon which Muang Tam was built slopes ever so gently from south east to north west. Streams originating in the low hills to the southeast of Muang Tam enter the reservoir on its south-eastern corner. From the northern corners of the reservoir openings allow the stored water to flow down to the massive Khlong Pun, or 'Lime Canal' dug across the valley floor. While the course of this canal has now begun to meander, its unnatural straightness in the level landscape shows that it was originally built by man.

The canal is perfectly sited at the lowest point of the basin formed between the Khao Phnom Rung, over 300 metres high, and the 250 metre-high hills to the south of Muang Tam. Numerous streams which bring the water off the slopes of Phnom Rung are also channelled by man-made trenches into the Sa Bua Lai baray lying at the eastern foot of Khao Phnom Rung, and the Khlong Pun. The canal stretches for over 20 kilometres, from the south side of the Phnom Rung mountain, north east to the nearest town.

Altogether, the system includes at least thirty to forty kilometres of canals, two large baray, and fifteen small basins. The men, women, and children whose lives were spent caring for the temples, were also responsible for the construction, maintenance, and operation of water as well.

On aerial photographs, the remains of small canals branching off the central conduit, form a criss-cross pattern on the level floodplain. This method of water management offered protection against the unpredictable pattern of rainfall that the farmers had to cope with. If the spring rains came late, the young rice seedlings might die. If at the end of August, as was often the case, the rains suddenly ceased, water could be drawn from baray. Likewise, if the September and October rains proved too heavy, water could be drawn off to the level needed to ensure a successful harvest. Given assurance of water from these water control structures of the temples, the region could prosper.

During recent excavations in and around the baray, a male stone figure was found, carved from the same sandstone as that found earlier within the enclosure of Muang Tam and also of comparable size. In addition his clothes and ornaments are similar. The only differences are in the hair styles and importantly in the small fangs which can be clearly seen at the corners of his mouth. Accordingly this figure can unequivocally be identified as a Mahakala guardian figure which would have stood as a pair with the Nandikesvara. The latter would have stood on the left and the Mahakala on the right (seen from our view point). We do not know why this and the other guardian (right) were moved from their original position. Possibly this was due to a change in religion, or for some other reason. (National Museum, Bangkok)

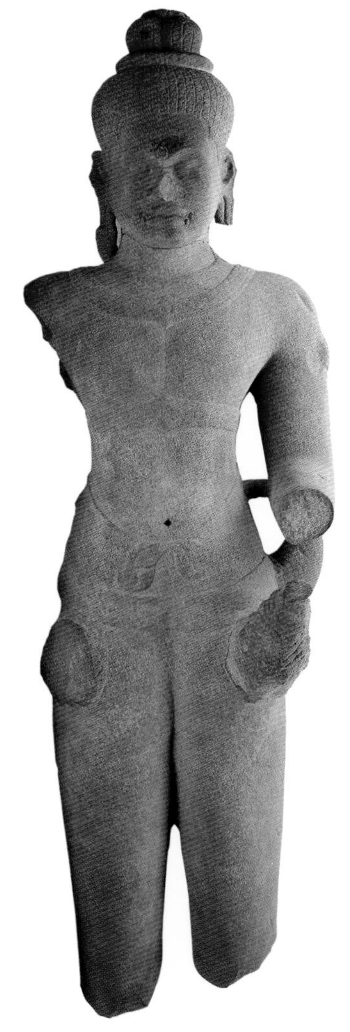

During excavations at Muang Tam a stone sculpture of a standing male figure was found near the base of the eastern gopura broken into three separate pieces - head, torso and legs. The statue's hair is gathered into a chignon and held in place by a circlet. His face is calm with a hint of a smile. He wears a sampot gathered below his navel, but the folds have not yet been carved. It is girdled with a cloth belt. Another indication that the statue is unfinished is the raised stone ovals on the thighs. These would have supported the arms during carving, to be carefully chiselled away at the end. The style of the piece places it firmly in the Baphuon period. It has been suggested that the figure represents Shiva in his human form, but this seems unlikely as a large linga has already been found in the main prang and this figure is probably that of a guardian. If this it correct, the arms, which have not yet been found, would have been in the position of holding a club. Thus all in all it would seem that this figure is a Nandikesvara. (National Museum, Bangkok)

Opposite
The eastern gopura to the outer enclosure. The east and west gopuras to Muang Tam have three entrance doorways, while the north and south have only one. The central doorway (on the left) passes into a room of cruciform shape, while the two side entrances lead to a connecting rectangular chamber. This is the most highly finished of the four gopuras, although it seems as if none of the stone roofs were completed.

The outer lintel (left) and pediment (right) from the southern door of the outer eastern gopura. Both have been finely carved with the motifs and iconography popular in the beginning and middle of the 11th century, including the ubiquitous kala. In this eastern gopura art historians have identified two distinct styles which hitherto have been

attributed to two different periods; namely the inner lintel above the south door to the Khleang period and this lintel to the Baphuon period. It confirms that stylistic classification based on the Cambodian models does not necessarily apply in Thailand.

The pediment frames from the eastern gopura end in bald-headed nagas spewing forth garlands, characteristic of the Baphuon style.

The laterite walls of the outer enclosure average 2.75 metres. They are topped with a fine coping and are generally in good condition, although certain sections have become rather wavy and collapsed because of subsidence.

Subsidence has been a feature throughout the site. The gopuras and enclosure walls in particular have shifted and sunk. Here, gaps in the jointing of the sandstone blocks that form the wall of the eastern gopura attest to the weakening of the foundations.

Pilaster with floral decoration typical of the 11th century Baphuon style.

Overleaf
Within the outer enclosure is a moat which has been cut by four broad walkways and thus effectively turned into four L-shaped ponds. Each is surrounded by laterite steps surmounted by the stone body of a five-headed naga. This view from the south-east corner clearly shows the Baphuon interpretation of the naga.

Nagas surround each of the four ponds and their tails frame stone gates which open onto steps leading down to the water. The setting as a whole with its concentric enclosures suggests that the ponds were considered sacred, symbolizing the four oceans surrounding Mount Meru. A similar arrangement has not been found elsewhere, even in Cambodia.

Outer lintel of the eastern gopura of the gallery. This illustrates example the mix of Khmer styles applied concurrently at Muang Tam. The lintel resembles those found at the Royal Palace of Angkor which date to the Khleang period. However, this lintel cannot be dated to the Khleang because it must have been carved after the construction of main towers in the 11th century.

The inner lintel of the inner eastern gopura. This lintel portrays a scene which was extremely popular in the 11th century, that of Krishna subduing the Naga Kaliya.

Overleaf: *the inner eastern gopura seen from the edge of the north-east pond. The rounded blocks in the foreground form the body of the naga.*

Opposite
The inner eastern gopura seen from the inner courtyard. The eastern, southern and northern gopuras of the inner gallery are constructed of sandstone to a cruciform plan, while the western gopura is rectangular in plan and was constructed of brick which has collapsed. All were probably roofed with brick. The gallery at Muang Tam may be compared with that at Sdok Kok Thom in that both have rows of windows on both the inner and outer walls and there are no corner pavilions. The lintel, temporarily placed in the foreground, features a kala topped by a deity, the whole surmounted by nine praying rishis.

The view over the inner courtyard towards the inner eastern gopura from the southern gopura. In the courtyard in front of the prasat can be seen the brick bases of the two 'libraries'. Both face west towards the towers. This arrangement, including the group of prangs, is similar to that at Prasat Kamphaeng Yai. In the foreground, the eye and mouth of a makara decorate one of the southern gopura's sandstone blocks.

Above *The inner southern gopura.*

Overleaf *A view of the central prangs before restoration. Visible here are the outer prangs of the front row and the northern prang of the back row. All five prangs stand on a single low laterite base facing east and originally the central prang of the front row was the largest.*

Colonette from the door frame of the northern prang, front row. Although overall the carving is in Baphuon style, here the flower pattern is enclosed in a square instead of the more usual diamond shape.

Lintel from the northern prang, front row, showing Umamahesvara. The Baphuon style lintel showing Shiva and Uma riding the bull Nandin, in situ on the northern prang of the front row, contrasts with the other lintels at Muang Tam in its execution. The naive treatment of the figures, not without charm, shows the influence of local folk art. The row of rishis seated on the backs of the nagas is found on two other lintels at this temple.

The unfinished pediment from the south side of the northern prang, front row. The corners have been carved with the rough outline of a naga, while the pediment frame is designed as a curved inverted U shape.

Opposite
Looking back from the northern gopura.

Right
Base of a door frame colonette showing praying rishis at the outer entrance of the inner eastern gopura.

Overleaf
The prangs after restoration, from the west. The pediments are well-carved but lack detail and it is possible that originally they were decorated with stucco relief. (Traces of stucco have been discovered while excavating and restoring the main prang and so it is quite likely that the other four may also have had such decoration.)

Above *The view back to the ponds and central prang from the outer western gopura. All of these gopuras have finely carved windows decorated with balusters, as can be seen at right.*

Opposite *The outside of the western outer gopura. Note the uncarved lintel above the side entrance showing how only the surface has been prepared. One of the pilasters has merely had a design roughed out while the other has been partially carved. The unfinished pilasters allow us to study the carving techniques and show that the entire scene would first be roughed out after which carving would begin. However, there seems to have been no fixed rule about which part of the stone would be worked first, with sometimes carving begining from the top down and vice versa. It must have been up to the individual, as examples exist of various ways of working. Above the door frames, or the structural lintels, of each entrance the craftsmen have constructed a careful arch, and the sandstone used is of the highest quality.*

Approximately 100 metres to the north of the prasat is a large baray, one of the few that have not dried up in the centuries since it was built. Extending on an east-west axis, this baray is approximately one kilometre long and half a kilometre wide and it must have been constructed for the use of the local population. From an inscription found at Sdok Kok

Thom it can be established that all the various barays, apart from those specifically constructed for a particular religious site, were intended to be used for the benefit of the local populace. It was originally surrounded with laterite in the form of steps leading down to the lake. This has now all disappeared.

PRASAT SDOK KOK THOM

ปราสาทสด๊อกก๊อกธม

Opposite
The eastern gopura from inside the remains of the north-east 'library'. Its superstructure is stepped in a manner typical of gopuras in Cambodia from the beginning of the Angkorean period on. The majority of Baphuon gopuras are cruciform in plan with a stepped roof, but in Thailand this is the only example. The two other Khmer temples in Thailand conforming to this form, at Prasat Muang Singh (Kanchanaburi), and Prasat Wat Kamphaeng Laeng (Phetchaburi) are from the later Bayon period during the reign of King Jayavarman VII (13th century). Elsewhere in Thailand, cruciform gopuras merely have a vaulted rather than a stepped prasat-style roof.

Below
Stele found in the gallery of the enclosure. (National Museum, Bangkok)

This small Baphuon period temple is situated 33 kilometres north of Aranyaprathet by road in the Ta Phraya district of Prachinburi province. It was build during the reign of King Udayadityavarman II in the 11th centruy. Right on the border, Sdok Kok Thom was for a number of years in the 1980s occupied as a military post by the KPNLF troops and therefore unvisitable. It was 'opened' when Thai troops pushed back the Cambodian rebels and began clearing the mines in 1990 for a visit by HRH Princess Maha Chakri Sirindhorn. A relatively compact site, Sdok Kok Thom retains a fairly complete gopura at the main east entrance, enclosure wall and 'libraries', while its prang has collapsed, in an unusual way, leaving the west side as a thin spire. The rubble of fallen sandstone blocks surrounds the prang.

Despite its modest size, the relative importance of the priestly family who had been given the site by King Udayadityavarman II led to the consecration of an important Shiva linga, with a stele being inscribed in Sanskrit to commemorate the event. Indeed, Sdok Kok Thom is best known for its inscription, one of the most important for the study of Khmer history. Now housed in the National Museum in Bangkok, it dates to about 1052, during the reign of Udayadityavarman II and chronicles the history of the Shivakaivalya dynasty of priests who had served King Jayavarman II, founder of the Khmer empire, since 802. It relates how Jayavarman II arrived from Java, became king of Indrapura (probably east and across the Mekhong river from present-day Phnom Penh) and later moved his capital to Hariharalaya, close to Angkor on the northern shore of the Tonlé Sap. In addition it also provides information on subsequent Khmer history, the Khmer system of kingship, the various beliefs adhered to and details about the Brahmin family and their involvement with later Khmer kings.

The south-eastern 'library', from the south. As in most Khmer temples there are a pair situated in front of the main prang. The particular feature of these two is that large windows pierce each side.

A gallery extends from either side of the gopura, and is similar to that at Phnom Wan. Dating from the late 11th century, it is composed of a row of window frames both on the outside and inside. It is possible that the roof was wood framed with tiles on top.

The main prang collapsed a long time ago and all that remains is the western wall, which is in a bad state of decay. What we can see today is the wall up to slightly above the cornice. The false doors on the western and southern side remain but the base has disappeared because the stone has been pushed out. Nevertheless it is possible to imagine the former importance and size of this prasat reflecting the wealth and stature of the Brahmin family which built it.

PRASAT BAN PHLUANG

ปราสาทบ้านพลวง

Opposite
Ban Phluang is constructed on a relatively high, three-lobed laterite base, whose wings extend a great deal at the sides and at the front leading to the conclusion that originally further structures may have been planned.

Situated in the Prasat district of Surin province, the small Baphuon temple of Ban Phluang rests pristinely upon its base within a landscaped courtyard. A moat, crossed by a single causeway on the east side, surrounds the sanctuary. Like so many of the Khmer temples in Thailand, the tranquility and order seen at Ban Phluang today is the result of years of careful reconstruction and continued maintenance by the Fine Arts Department. Reconstruction work was carried out at Ban Phluang during the 1970s by Vance Childress, an American architect working in conjunction with the Fine Arts Department. This extremely detailed excavation report offers valuable insights into Khmer construction techniques in general. Here, all three building materials were employed - sandstone, laterite and brick. Both laterite and brick were easily obtained locally, but most probably the sandstone was brought from quarries to the south. Its transportation was not a problem, for most of the pieces weighed less than a 1,000 pounds, similar to loads of rice carried on ox-carts today.

Prasat Ban Phluang was built during the second half of the 11th century. At this time, Udayadityavarman II (1055-1065) ruled at Angkor. The style of architecture and sculpture of this period takes its name from the Baphuon, the major temple built by Udayadityavarman II at Angkor. During this period, the Khmer interpretation of the pyramid temple-mountain with terraces and concentric galleries developed greater complexity. An evolution in decorative carving was also seen, particularly in the depiction of the human figure and the appearance of greater narration on lintel carvings.

Finds of pottery underneath nearly all the houses of the present village at Ban Phluang show that the 11th century village occupied much the same area as today. Whether an earlier village existed at the site is unknown. The lack of inscriptions from the site means that the name of the ruler who initiated construction of the temple also remains a mystery. The temple's reservoir or baray was once almost a kilometre in length. Construction of a reservoir was often the first step in the founding of a new village, for the water provided an essential resource to cope with the extended dry season, ensuring a food supply for the people.

The building of the temple, although begun in the mid-11th century, was never completed, perhaps reflecting the financial situation of the time, or the relative power of the person who commissioned it. During excavations, two unfinished naga cornices were unearthed. Among the several guardian figures carved on the outside of the lower part of the temple, one has been left unfinished and the chisel marks left by the sculptor can still be seen. A number of the tools used to build Ban Phluang were found during excavations. These included the iron chisels and mallets that were used to work the sandstone and laterite. Although such implements tend to shatter aged stone, both the sandstone and laterite are softer for at least a couple of years after quarrying.

The construction of the temple started with the laterite foundation, perhaps on the auspicious north-eastern corner. The blocks were placed evenly on a prepared bed of sand, with precautions taken to ensure that all pieces were smooth. Notches found on both the front and back of the bottom of blocks show that a system of lifting was used to place the four levels, each about half a metre high. A different placement method was used to lay the floor of the terrace, for these blocks have holes not on the bottom edge, but one on the top and one midway on the back of the block. This would have allowed each piece to be swung snugly into place against its neighbours and ensure a good fit.

Careful analysis of dimensions during excavation at Ban Phluang showed that the next step in the construction of the temple was the installation of the pedestal and linga dedicating the sanctuary to Shiva. Essential astrological materials would have been placed under the pedestal, along with precious stones, gold leaf, and valued spices. Looting, however, probably began at the temple as early as the 14th century. Robbers attempted to remove the pedestal, and dug down to a depth of almost four metres in search of treasures placed during consecration.

Following the placement of this ritual centre of the temple, the sandstone base of the temple was laid. This exterior was faced with laterite on the inside. Doors were constructed on all four sides, although only the east door provided entry into the temple, the doors on the other sides being false. Stones were probably moved up onto the terrace platform on ramps, and scaffolding set up as the bulding grew higher. Once a stone had been set roughly in position, it may have been lifted again. Holes drilled into the top of the block would have been first filled with water. Wooden pegs inserted into the holes would become tight once they absorbed the water. Ropes could then be wrapped around the pegs, and with the aid of a simple pulley, it could be raised. This would allow a final finishing of the sides and bottom to obtain a good fit. Some stones are better nested than others, as both beginner and seasoned artisans would have been working on the temple.

After 18 levels of sandstone, the builders probably switched to brick. The use of brick to create the upper layers of a sandstone tower is an unusual feature of the temple. It may have stemmed from difficulties in obtaining stone, or the easier logistics of placing the bricks on the upper portions of the tower. During excavation, large quantities of brick were unearthed in the area around the temple, and the top layer of sandstone was found to have been inscribed with brick shapes. It is not certain, however, if the tower was ever finished. The other unfinished elements such as the guardian figures suggest that work may have been abruptly interrupted, perhaps due to a change in fortune of the local patron, or the ruler at Angkor.

The eastern lintel shows Indra riding a single-headed Airavata. It is widely known that Indra is the god who protected the eastern side and accordingly representations of Indra are frequently found on that side of buildings, whether carved on lintels or pediments. The god is invariably seated on his personal steed, the elephant Airavata, sometimes shown with three heads and sometimes simply with one. However, at Ban Phluang it would appear that special prominence has been given to Indra, as not only does he appear on this lintel as usual, but also on the northern pediment and the southern lintel. Such representations are exceptional and differ from other comparable structures.

Two of the guardians carved on the south-west corner of the temple. Although they are not completely finished, the position of their hands enables them to be dated firmly to the 11th centruy.

The eastern pediment showing Krishna Govardhana, or Krishna lifting the Govardhana mountain in order to protect the herdsmen and the cattle from the might of Indra's rain. Such a representation, with Krishna as the victor and Indra as the vanquished, would seem to be iconographically opposed to the representations of Indra discussed above and to date no satisfactory explanation for such conflicting iconography has been found.

As at Muang Tam, a mixture of styles can be found here, within the same pediment from the south side of the prang. Thus although the temple dates to the 11th century, a detail of the pediment end continues to show nagas with Khleang characteristics albeit carved in a later period. However, the middle part of the pediment (opposite) with a kala surmounted by a deity is typical of the Baphuon period.

Overleaf
The fact that the temple is constructed from sandstone on a laterite base and is comparatively high, suggests that its builder was a relatively powerful individual and the reason why the prasat was only completed to cornice level may be due to a dearth of suitable sandstone in the surrounding area. Alternatively there may have been a financial problem, as the fact that the cornice is evenly levelled off suggests that there was never a sandstone top to the structure (if there had been and this had toppled down, one would have expected to find certain segments scattered in the vicinity as is the case in the small prang of Phnom Rung). In addition, the building techniques employed with such structures usually required that the whole be completed before any carving began. The only other possibility is that the upper part may have been built from wood or, as here, brick, both of which would have been widely available and relatively cheap. However, further evidence to support the theory that the prasat is unfinished is the fact that the figures on either side of the entrance and the floral decoration are incompletely carved.

PRASAT NARAI JAENG WAENG

ปราสาทนารายณ์เจงเวง

Opposite
The eastern pediment has been crudely roofed over at a later stage. Above the entrance porch on the eastern side, the pediment shows a 12-armed dancing Shiva, which makes an unusual comparison with contemporary representations found elsewhere. At Phimai and Phnom Rung, Shiva has 10 arms. Nevertheless, the surrounding iconography is typical. On Shiva's left (our right) a group of deities includes Ganesha playing a musical instrument on the far right, while on the other side is a representation of Shiva's disciple, Kareikkal-ammeyar, seated at Shiva's feet with another figure. Sometimes if the Vishnu-like figure has four arms and is not carrying his attributes but is playing musical instruments, the carving may in fact represent Nandin in his human form known as Nandikesvara. Normally Nandin the bull appears as Shiva's steed, but ancient chronicles relate that as Nandikesvara he would play musical instruments while Shiva danced. Kareikkal-ammeyar existed during the 6th or 7th century as a faithful disciple. From the 8th century onwards she began to appear in Southern Indian art, and in the 11th and early 12th centuries she became very popular in Khmer art, after which she does not appear again.

Situated in the Muang district of Sakhon Nakhon province, this small prasat in the Baphuon style probably derives its name (Jaeng Waeng in Khmer means 'with long legs') from a carving of Vishnu (or Narai in Khmer and Thai) reclining on the northern pediment (see p. 219). The current name still utilises the ancient Khmer pronunciation, rather than the modern pronunciation of Cheung Waeng. This demonstrates that when the Lao fled to this area there were still some ancient Khmer speakers among them and the Lao thus adopted the Khmer name with the old system of pronunciation which has remained to this day. Later changes in Khmer pronunciation were not adopted for the temple as there were obviously no longer any Khmer speakers among the local population.

The prasat's only entrance is on the eastern side while the other three sides have false doors. The porch pediment is broken and only the porch lintel remains, on which is depicted Indra riding on Airavata.

The northern, southern and eastern lintels show varying treatments of the Baphuon style. The northern (above) and eastern (below) both show Krishna; in the northern example he fights one simha, in the eastern two. (The iconography of Krishna fighting simhas is unique to Khmer art, as in India he is only found fighting elephants.) Both also utilise the familiar centralised compostion in which Krishna is surrounded by deeply carved interlocking floral motifs.The southern lintel (opposite) employs a narrative technique, divided in two by a horizontal line. Unfortunately the main scene has not been deciphered, although the monkey under a porch in the upper level suggests the Ramayana.

The northern pediment showing Vishnu reclining. This representation of a reclining Vishnu (known as Vishnu Anantasayin Padmanabha), on the northern pediment, probably gave the temple its popular name. It compares interestingly with a similar scene at Kamphaeng Yai. Both would seem to have been carved by local workmen in a folk art style, as evidenced by the checked pattern of his sampot. One of Vishnu's four arms, his upper right, is used to support his head while his lower right arm is holding a baton. His lower left hand holds a lotus flower, while his upper left arm is not visible. Only the head of Brahma remains as his body has been destroyed. However, although Vishnu is featured in this pediment, the fact that the eastern - and more important - pediment shows the dancing Shiva suggests that this temple was dedicated to the latter deity.

The false entrance on the northern face has a fine somasutra with the head of a makara. The somasutra, of which very few examples remain in situ in Thailand, is a conduit through which lustral water which had been used in ceremonies inside the sanctuary passes outside. Here, the makara's snout is lifted up to resemble a trunk.

PRASAT SIKHORAPHUM

ปราสาทศรีขรภูมิ

Detail showing false door in the south-west tower.

Detail of pilaster capital showing curving foliage and a Garuda with wings outstreched.

The style of the lintels and other sandstone carvings of Prasat Sikhoraphum in the eponymous district of Surin province dates the monument to the Angkor Wat period in the early part of the 12th century, although the superstructure of the brick towers was rebuilt by the Lao at a later date. The plan of the temple is a quincunx with four brick towers around a central larger one surrounded by a moat. Such a plan is not found elsewhere in Thailand and has particular cosmological significance. Symbolism of this kind was normally reserved for more important state temples such as Ta Keo, Pre Rup and Angkor Wat.

The five towers sit upon a low, square laterite platform, oriented to the east. Brick was no longer used in Cambodia as a building material for prasats or important buildings after being supplanted by sandstone during the 11th century and if it was used at all it was only for insignificant buildings and for small additional details. But in Khmer architecture in Thailand, brick continued to be widely used in the construction of prasats until the second half of the 12th century, when laterite took over. However, as in Cambodia, for very important buildings sandstone was the preferred material from the 11th century onwards.

The importance of the site is also reflected in the care with which the brick was laid. The rebuilding by the Lao clearly show the results of craftsmen who, as well as coming from a different cultural background, did not understand the intricacies of Khmer architecture.The various antefixes have been repositioned at will with the deities responsible for the various directions (north, south, etc) being replaced incorrectly.

Today, the most significant feature of the site is the sandstone doorway with its pilasters, lintels and columns still intact. Little decoration remains on the four smaller towers, but the vestiges still in place suggest a prosperous establishment. At the end of an arch on the south-west tower, a multi-headed naga raises his heads in protection. The nagas emerge from the square and toothy jaws of a makara. The creature lacks the snout usually associated with the makara, resembling instead the sleek lines of the dragons seen on the lintel over the doorway of the central tower. Remnants of stucco can be seen on the brick beneath the nagas. Stucco motifs were also found by the Fine Arts Department during recent excavations at Muang Tam, to the south-west of Prasat Sikhoraphum, a reminder that all the brick towers were once coated and most probably painted.

Apart from the 10-armed dancing Shiva, the four other deities from left to right are: Shiva's consort Uma, here appearing as Durga and holding a human-headed sceptre; a four-armed Vishnu; Brahma playing the cymbals; and finally, Ganesha, Shiva's son, playing the drums. The upper level shows, at left, the Kiratarjuna story from the Mahabharata epic, while the scene in the upper right remains unidentified. The garland's foliage swirls into curves across the base of the lintel. Within these waves are six small figures, each riding a crested dragon. Only the upper part of the dragon can be seen, but each is carefully segmented, front paws raised as if to mount the incline.

Detail opposite *Three small hamsa birds support Shiva's pedestal, and signify by their presence, the celestial location of the dance. They stand proudly with beaks raised and small wings outstretched from the feathers of their plump bodies. Their oversized feet rest on the crown of a kala, whose hands grasp the lower legs of two rampant male lions, bearing aloft the lintel's garland.*

These nagas on the pediment angle of the main prang appears to date from the preceding Baphuon period. As discussed previously, this again calls into question the validity of applying the Cambodian dating system to this part of the Khmer empire.

The pilasters flanking the main doorway of the central prang are carved with two figures. The inner sides bear the figure of a guardian who may be Nandikesvara, holding a club. The outer faces are each carved with the figure of an apsara, or devata - one of only two instances known in Thailand. Their hair, clothes, poise and even the parrots perched by their shoulders are typical of the Angkor Wat period. As in similar Cambodian examples note the awkward stylized placement of the feet.

Overleaf
This arrangement of the towers in a quincunx on a low base is unique in Khmer architecture. The brick superstructure was rebuilt by the Lao in the 15th to 16th centuries.

PRASAT YAI NGAO

ปราสาทยายเหงา

Situated in the Sangkhla district of Surin province, this prasat dating from the Angkor Wat period of the 12th century, otherwise known as Don Ngao (de Lajonquière), consists of two brick prangs on low laterite bases. In fact one would expect to find three prangs in which the central would be the largest. However, for whatever reason, only the main prang and the smaller northern one were completed, and there is no sign at all of building work even having commenced on the southern structure - only the site was cleared in preparation.

Both prangs face east and have a single entrance on that side, the other three sides having the usual false doors. Above these there must have originally been quite deep projecting porches but only traces can still be seen of the holes bored to receive the wooden roof frame and other marks on the walls.

Today the area surrounding the prasat is used by Buddhist monks for religious purposes. Excavations by the Fine Arts Department in the area surrounding the prasat have revealed various artefacts such as antefixes in the shape of nagas surmounted by Garudas.

Right
The makara-naga arch on the southern pediment of the main prang is a fine example of Angkor Wat style carving, unusually executed in brick. This medium would probably account for the carving being shallower than contemporary sandstone equivalents.

Far right
The capital of the column supporting this arch is uncarved but shows the exceptionally close jointing of the brickwork.

PRASAT PHIMAI

ปราสาทหินพิมาย

Opposite
The sanctuary from the north-west corner of the inner courtyard. The roofs at Phimai are significant in that they are curved in shape. This represented a major change for Khmer architecture, both in constructional and visual terms.

The principal Khmer temple on the Khorat plateau at Phimai is about 70 kilometres north-east of Nakhon Ratchasima and bounded by rivers on three sides. The most important of these is the Mun River, which turns southward at this point. A old tributary of the Mun also branches off to partially enclose the old mound upon which the temple was built. The natural protection offered by the rivers has long made it an attractive habitation site. During reconstruction of the temple in the 1960s a brick structure was found to underlie the present sandstone temple. As well as using different materials, the earlier building had a different orientation than the south-facing complex does today. Black burnished pottery found in association with this previous phase of occupation has been dated to approximately 500 AD. Archaeological survey and excavation of surrounding sites has yielded similar pottery, along with evidence of still earlier occupation.

Due to the presence of several converging rivers, a wide floodplain has been formed through deposition of alluvium. From prehistoric times, the people of Phimai have established communities on slight rises in this floodplain, naturally occurring mounds formed through downcutting of the rivers and aeolian action. During the monsoon rains from May to October, water runs off the village mound and collects in the lower-lying perimeter area and the ricefields beyond. In a number of cases, the natural pooling of water around the mound has been enhanced through excavation of a moat. This allows drainage of excess water during floodtime, and conservation of water during the long and unpredictable dry season from November to March.

The religion of the pre-Khmer temples at Phimai remains uncertain. Animistic worship was important, and some shrines may have been built by Buddhist devotees. According to Prince Damrong, a Wheel of the Law was found together with a Buddha image in the Dvaravati style. A platform excavated in a mound south of the city gates had four large pots embedded in the corners, suggesting it was used for ritual purposes. It is likely that a number of religions were practised simultaneously, with an intermixing of animistic, Buddhist, and Hindu cults.

Thus during many centuries prior to the first inscriptions erected at Phimai, the natural advantages of the site encouraged a tradition of settlement and worship which by 1000 AD represented a considerable heritage. The earliest inscription in the Phimai area written in both Sanskrit and Khmer was installed at Prasat Phnom Wan, located to the

south of Phimai, in 1082 (see p.104). It commands the military and religious officials of a king called Jayavarman VI, 'victorious protector', to care for the monastery dedicated to Shiva at Phnom Wan. The inscription also mentions Vimayapura, the city of Vimaya (Phimai). A monastery is thought to have existed at Phimai also - one which was kept active within the temple walls well into this century. The real significance of the inscription is that the ruling line of Jayavarman VI, known as the Mahidharapura dynasty, is thought to have originated in this part of Northeast Thailand. The presence of so many major temples - Phnom Rung, Muang Tam, Phimai, Phnom Wan - in this region corroborates this belief. A descendant of Jayavarman VI was Suryavarman II (1113-1150), one of the greatest Khmer kings who expanded the empire to its limits and built Angkor Wat. He was also kinsman to Narendraditya of Phnom Rung, and the royal connections of this area are reflected in the size and importance of Phimai and Phnom Rung.

Several inscriptions have been found at Phimai itself, and have been the subject of considerable scholarly analysis. One of these was found on the south gopura of the inner enclosure around the central temple. This inscription carries several dates, the last of which is 1112 AD. The local ruler, Virendradhipativarman, is mentioned not only in this inscription, but can be seen in the bas-reliefs of Angkor Wat. There he rides on his war elephant, accompanied by his troops, in a similar scene to the victory narratives carved on the lintels at Phnom Rung.

Another parallel to Phnom Rung can be seen in Virendradhipativarman's efforts to establish his importance both to his subjects and those to whom he paid tribute at Angkor. As was often customary, he did this through his installation of an image identified simultaneously with the god and with himself as ruler. In this case the image was of a Mahayanist deity known as Trailokyavijaya. This Tantric god is an emanation of a Bodhisattva who has assumed this form to convert the Hindu god Shiva. The inscription refers to the image of Trailokyavijaya as senapati or general of the Lord of Vimaya.

The meaning of the name Vimaya remains unclear, opinons ranging from Indonesian connections to various manifestations of the Buddha. Most interpretations point towards a Mahayanist origin, and may also be understood as a resurgence of pre-existing cults. Evidence for this includes a pre-Angkorean (pre-9th century) inscription dedicating a Buddhist image. The stone upon which the inscription was carved was reused at a later date when the first or inner gallery of the temple complex was erected. In this context, the consecration of a Tantric image was Virendradhipativarman's declaration to Angkor of the independent heritage and economic importance of the Phimai region. Ties of vassalage were reciprocal. For example, the ruler at Phimai contributed manpower to Angkorean campaigns, territory to the Khmer controlled lands, and the products of the Northeast. He in turn received support for the foundation of the temple, in the form of priestly functions, artisans, and protection if need arose.

Whatever the origin of Mahayana Buddhism at Phimai, its presence at a major Khmer temple of the beginning of the 12th century was unusual. In Cambodia at this time the principal religion was still Hinduism, but here on the Khorat plateau, the Khmer form of Mahayana Buddhism had been well-established since the 7th century. Evidence of this may be deduced from the many Buddha images found here and in the neighbouring province of Buriram. It did not affect the plan of the temple, but as we will see, encouraged a number of unique motifs.

Plan of the Temple

Although the main road from Nakhon Ratchasima to Phimai enters the town on the north, the ancient temple faces south south-east. Some scholars speculate that this southern orientation may reflect the influence of an earlier kingdom to the south, recorded in Chinese annals as Funan. The Chinese were active in maritime trade during the time of Funan, about the 1st to 5th century AD, and it is possible that the Chinese custom of southern orientation was conveyed to Funan. Yet another speculation suggests that Jayavarman VI orientated the temple in honour of his ancestors - south being the direction reserved for ancestral worship. It is also the direction of Angkor.

To enter the old town, it is necessary to travel through modern Phimai, to the ancient laterite landing stage which crosses the river about one kilometre to the south. The landing stage, which is said to be the bathing place of the heroine in a local legend, is one of the few remaining non-religious stone structures. It serves as a reminder of the advantageous location of the site, at the confluence of the many navigable waterways.

Proceeding north, one passes through the main city gates, recently reconstructed by the Fine Arts Department. Known as Pratu Chai, or 'victory gate', this sandstone and laterite southern entry is wide enough to accomodate the passage of an elephant. Gates can also be seen on the north and west of the town wall, a rectangular enclosure of about half a kilometre east to west and a kilometre north to south. The eastern gate has since been eroded by the Mun River, but all of these gates and the city wall were added during the reign of Jayavarman VII. Within the town boundaries, an ancient village once stood, a pattern maintained by modern Phimai.

The entrance to the temple courtyard is marked by a cruciform naga terrace, now reconstructed by the Fine Arts Department. To the left of the cruciform terrace, is a large rectangular building dated to the end of the 12th century, the reign of King Jayavarman VII (1181-1219), commonly referred to as a storehouse (khleang). Sandstone grindstones have been excavated from the pavillion, which may have been used by brahmin priests to make ritual preparations.

The southern entrance gopura, built of sandstone, is the largest of the four gopuras which break the outer wall. The gate has three parts, the first marked by a pair of large square pillars flanked by balustraded windows. More pillars are seen in the second section, an imposing and monumental feature. To the left and right are additional

Overleaf
At the end of the causeway leading from the southern entrance, an inner gopura breaks the red sandstone gallery that surrounds the central courtyard.

The unrestored prang and inner gallery seen from the broken causeway leading from the southern entrance. Photographed c.1915.

This lintel, currently above the entrance door to the central courtyard, is not in its original position. Dating from the beginning of the Angkor Wat period, it retains a characteristic Baphuon arrangement of elements, although other features are not at all typical of that period. The giant holding two elephants above the kala is unusually fierce and large, but it is not possible to establish his identity.

porches, each divided into three rooms. The plan of the southern wing is repeated on the north, where it leads into the outer courtyard. Phimai's concentric plan now becomes apparent - the cosmological arrangement found in so many major Khmer temples. The outer wall forms a rectangle enclosing a courtyard. This, with four large ponds, one in each corner, surrounds an inner gallery with gopuras. This in turn encloses the inner courtyard at the heart of which is the sanctuary and its prang. A causeway leads towards this central complex from the outer entrance gopura. Two nearly square stone pavilions can be seen to the left, near the outer west gopura. These were recently excavated and reconstructed by the Fine Arts Department. Their function is as yet unknown.

The inner gallery at Phimai forms a rectangle around the inner courtyard. It was in this gallery that the pre-Angkorean Buddhist inscription was found. The gallery is continuous, unlike the partitioned gallery at Phnom Rung. It may be entered through four gopuras, one on each side aligned with the entrances to the prang, offset a little to the north of the courtyard as a whole. Therefore from the doorway of the western gopura one may look through the sanctuary and on to the gopura on the east.

The construction of the central sandstone prang and the surrounding gallery are the earliest parts of the sanctuary as it is seen today. Construction of these parts began during the reign of Jayavarman VI (1080-1107) but was probably completed under his successor, Dharanindravarman I (1107-1112).

The gopuras have stairs to enter the gallery, which is raised almost a metre above ground level. The gallery is made of red sandstone, a softer type of stone than the white sandstone. Many of the blocks have developed black areas on the surface, a result of weathering often called 'desert varnish'. The galleries consist of two walls and a corbelled roof. Unlike contemporaneous temples in Burma, the Khmer never mastered the technique of a true arch, thus limiting both the width and height of arched elements in their architecture. Much of the roof over the inner gallery has collapsed, in part because of this construction technique and in part because of the softness of the red sandstone.

On the western side of the inner courtyard to the north and south are two prangs dated to the end of the 12th century, the same period of buiding activity under King Jayavarman VII which saw the construction of the pavilion or hospital outside the temple's southern gate. These are known as Prang Brahmadat and Prang Hin Daeng.

Prang Brahmadat is built of laterite blocks forming a redented square tower, some 16 metres high. The building has a similar profile to the main sanctuary, but does not appear to have ever been finished. Three freestanding statues were found in Prang Brahmadat, the most important of which is thought to be a portrait of King Jayavarman VII (see p. 242). This stone figure, 1.42 metres high, is now kept in the National Museum in Bangkok. It is unusual in that although the right leg rests upon the left in the meditational position of the Buddha, the face and torso are clearly modelled from life rather than the more usual stylized Buddha's face. A similar statue, a portrait of Jayavarman VII at a somewhat younger age, was found at Krol Romeas (Angkor Thom).

This sandstone carving, 1.13 metres high, was described by the French scholar George Cœdès as depicting a portly man with his hair drawn up onto the top of his head into a small chignon, a hairstyle which suggests a portrait of a man rather than a god. The same person is depicted on bas-relief scenes from the Bayon and Banteay Chmar, two major temples also dated to the time of Jayavarman VII. Many Khmer statues were undoubtedly modelled after actual people, as a glance at the Khmer peoples of Northeast Thailand today will confirm. However, nowhere else in Khmer art does there exist a group of sculptures which can be linked to one of the most powerful rulers of the Khmer Empire.

Prang Hin Daeng, 'red stone tower', is also square, built of red sandstone. The 15 metre high tower was built during the reign of Jayavarman VII, although the reversed position of some of the carved stones suggest that it may have incorporated material from an earlier structure. Behind Prang Hin Daeng is another laterite structure dated to the end of the 12th century. As several small lingas were found here during reconstruction, this building is commonly known as the Hindu shrine.

The main sanctuary, built of white sandstone, is over 32 metres long. Its plan is similar to Phnom Rung, consisting of a garbhagrha, antarala, and mandapa. The tower above the central cell rises in tiers, crowned by a lotus bud decoration. The elegantly proportioned prang represents a major departure in Khmer architectural style. It is possible that Phimai was the first temple to feature such a prominent curving tower and if so this prang would have been a model for the famous towers of Angkor Wat. The change was achieved by concealing the stepped effect with overhangs and corner antefixes. The sanctuary is also notable for its high base and the skilful interplay of the various levels. Many of the lintels above the doorways to the sanctuary depict Buddhist motifs which make Phimai unique. The Buddhist themes are particularly seen on the doors around and approaching the main shrine.

The southern lintel, for example, shows the Buddha meditating. He is sheltered under the seven hoods of the naga Muchalinda, with the serpent's body coiled round to raise the Buddha above the floodwaters. Over a door on the corridor leading to the southern antechamber is another scene from the life of the historical Buddha, the subduing of the evil forces of Mara. The Buddha can be seen in the centre of the lintel, seated on a lotus. The assault of Mara's army is depicted in the lower register. Two elephants raise their trunks towards the Buddha, the four-headed warriors on their heads straining upwards to attack. Some scholars believe that the depiction of these figures follows Tantric Mahayana Buddhist scripture.

Other animals act as mounts for Mara's soldiers, including several Chinese-inspired dragons similar to that seen on the eastern lintel at Phnom Rung. A hamsa, the goose who acts as a mount for the Hindu god Brahma, is carved on the right of the lintel. In the upper register, the daughters of Mara stand, a final temptation to test the Buddha. The most significant aspect of the lintel is the gesture of the Buddha. The figure is seated in the virasana position the right leg resting flat on the left. His right hand rests upon his bent knee, with his fingers extended to touch the ground, calling the earth to witness his virtue. The earth goddess, Dharani, responds by rising up and wringing out her long hair, wet with the accumulated waters of the Buddha's offerings. The waters wash away the army of Mara, and Buddha reigns supreme. This carving is dated stylistically to the early 12th century AD. It is thought to be the earliest representation of this gesture, one whose popularity continues today.

Several other lintels depict narrative scenes inspired by Buddhism. On the western side is a lintel whose central figure is the Buddha, both hands raised in the teaching or vitarka mudra gesture. The symmetrical style of his robe reflects that of the Mon-inspired 9th to 11th century Dvaravati art of the region. The Buddha's head, now sadly missing, was topped by a crown. On a lintel to the north of the main shrine, the central figure has three faces and six arms. He is surrounded by dancers who tread on human bodies, possibly the enemies of Buddhism. This figure has only tentatively been identified as the Mahayanist Vajrasattva, for the deity does not carry the attributes usually seen. The Mahayana deity Trailokyavijaya is thought to be the central figure on a lintel on the eastern side, but again questions remain about his iconography.

Hindu Iconography

By no means all of the lintels at Phimai take their inspiration from Buddhism. Many of the narratives, especially in the inner enclosure, relate to Hindu deities, particularly Shiva and Vishnu. As at Phnom Rung, the pediment over the main entry depicts Shiva dancing. However, the god Vishnu appears to have also been popular, particularly in his manifestation as Rama and Krishna. In the Krishna story, at the end of the period just before the present era, demons threatened the order of the cosmos. The goddess Earth ascended to the home of the gods, Mount Meru, and pleaded for protection. Chief among the demons was Kamsa, whom Vishnu had previously slain, but who had returned to cause havoc on earth. Vishnu was approached, and listened to the petition. He responded by plucking two hairs from his head, one fair and one dark. The two hairs became the half-brothers Krishna and Balarama, born to kill again the demon Kamsa. The two boys spent their childhood amongst cowherds, tending the flock.

Krishna's superhuman nature was at last revealed when he overcame a wicked naga king called Kaliya. Krishna tears the naga apart, jumps in the water, battles with the creature, and finally dances upon it. The great serpent eventually retreated, for Vishnu in all his guises is the moderating preserver, rather than destroyer. In his incarnation as Krishna, Vishnu defeats many other animals, including the bull Arishta, the horse Kesin, the elephant Kuvalayapida, and the simha. This last motif, although popular in Khmer scenes, does not actually figure in the Indian version of the tale. Krishna is usually seen gripping the rear leg of the animal as he prepares to hurl it into the air. Other times, such as on a lintel on the south-east entrance gopura, and another on the entry to the central courtyard, the taut torso of Krishna holds aloft two elephants whilst rampant lions issue from the mouth of the creature beneath his feet.

Opposite above
The main south entrance to the mandapa and the tower behind before restoration.

Opposite below
The Prang Brahmadat, north side, before restoration.

Above
The north elevation.
(Courtesy of Ecole Française d'Extrême Orient).

The final victory comes when Krishna kills the evil Kamsa. This episode is depicted on a lintel on the east porch of the central tower. In this lintel, and again and again in the carvings at Phimai, one is conscious of the surface of the stone in the bodies of the figures. There is a tension created by the contrast of the sharply tactile surface and the volumes confined within them. The rise of Krishna's chest as he raises his arms to assault Kamsa seems to push against the skin of the stone. The fixed outline of the lintel served to inspire rather than inhibit creativity, for it was within the rectangular and triangular confines of lintel and pediment that the Khmer love of narrative could be expressed. And within the narratives subscribed to during the 9th to 13th century AD, the divine human figure, the god who is king, reigned supreme. The manifestations were many, from small stationary guardians and ascetics, to the vibrant movements of dancing Shivas or Krishna defeating evil. Throughout Khmer art, until the excessive expansion and changing times which precipitated its disintegration after the reign of Jayavarman VII, the human figure mirrors the ascendancy of the individual. The ruler at the pinnacle of society, and the consequent multiplication of the hierachy beneath him, translated easily into the tales of valour from the Indian epics. The confidence and prosperity of Khmer culture reached its height during the 12th and 13th centuries. This is reflected at Phimai in the tensioned human figures; men and women who move amongst the riotous vegetation to fill the lintel's surface.

It seems fairly certain that this sculpture, found in the Prang Brahmadat, represents Jayavarman VII as it closely resembles the sculpture found at Krol Romeas, currently housed in the Phnom Penh museum. Other representations of the King have been found throughout the Khmer empire, among which the finest example is probably the head found at Kompong Svai. (National Museum, Bangkok)

This smaller Buddha under naga shares the same characteristics and style as the one opposite but the naga's hood and heads have disappeared. The presence of such Buddha images at Phimai show it to have been an important centre of Mahayana Tantric Buddhism. (National Museum, Bangkok)

This Buddha sheltered by naga is a very fine example of 13th century Bayon sculpture. His head shows the style clearly - his eyes are tightly closed, his expression has the hint of a smile, his hair is carved in rows of tight curls which reach a small peak on top instead of an aureole. An overall simplicity is apparent in the scupture as a whole in contrast to the typical Khmer love of ornamentation. His robe has all but disappeared with time and its presence has to be inferred from the stone filling the gap between his left arm and torso. In the Bayon period two types of Buddhas sheltered by nagas were carved, plain and ornamented, and this treatment of the space is typical of the unadorned type of Bayon Buddha. (Phimai Museum)

Left *Southern pediment from the mandapa, showing a 10-armed dancing Shiva.This variation on one of the classic themes of Khmer carving features the presence of Shiva's steed Nandin crouching at the extreme right and an unidentified deity on the opposite side next to Shiva's knee. This latter may represent Brahma riding on a hamsa. A headless Kareikkal-ammeyar with drooping breasts may just be discerned at the extreme left.*

Right *Pilaster detail from the southern side of the mandapa showing Vajrasattva. It would seem that towards the end of the 11th century and the beginning of the 12th the lower section of pilasters began to incorporate figurative carvings which served as guardian figures at entrances. Thus here at Phimai is a representation of Vajrasattva holding the thunderbolt and the bell and acting as a door guardian. Generally treatment of the lower portions of pilasters in the late Baphuon and Angkor Wat periods illustrate religious scenes.*

These naga pediment ends show the later Baphuon style in which the naga has a succession of curved incisions above its head topped by a foliate crown.

Opposite
Inner lintel from the northern porch of the prang, showing deities from Mahayana Buddhism. This lintel is divided into three parts with a central figure separating the two-tiered scenes to the left and right. This male figure with three faces and six arms is replicated in miniature by the four figures in the upper row. His first set of arms are folded in his lap in the meditation position, while two of his left hands seem to be holding bells whose tops are thunderbolts and his middle right hand holds a rosary. His meditation pedestal is decorated with the lotus petal pattern and below are a group of musicians. On both sides of the lower level are women dancing on bodies of men prostrating themselves. As with the central figure these are again replicated on the upper tier. It is difficult to interpret the complex iconography of the Tantric Mahayana Buddhism as embodied at Phimai. It is believed that the three-headed figure with six arms may represent Vajrasattva. However the items that he holds in his hands do not correspond with those usually associated with him. The dancing girls may represent yogini.

Pediment and lintel showing a scene from the Ramayana, from the western door of the mandapa. This scene from the Ramayana was carved both here and at Phnom Rung with a few small details differing between them. What is important and unusual in Khmer art is that here both the pediment and the lintel deal with the same story. The lintel shows that Rama and Lakshmana have been tied up by a naga in the form of a noose with Sita supporting Rama's head. The monkey troops are showing their sorrow with some of them pointing to Indrajit who is hidden in the clouds at the extreme right of the lintel and is in the posture of firing an arrow. The half-carved pediment above shows a Garuda flying down to help Rama and Lakshmana together with several simian soldiers.

The north-east corner of the main prang and the eastern door of the mandapa. From this north-eastern corner can be seen the doors of both the main prang and the mandapa.

Lintel from the eastern porch of the prang showing Krishna executing Kamsa. Early Angkor Wat style, early 12th century.
Various interpretations have been adduced for this scene. The most likely one would seem to be that of Krishna killing Kamsa. Here, Krishna appears in front of a tree, the top of which is an arch made up of the tails of two large birds. The couple Vasudeva and Devaki, father and mother of Krishna, are seated to Krishna's right. Krishna raises his right hand, which holds a club, while grasping Kamsa's topknot in his left. His left foot is raised in victory on the back of the prostrate Kamsa. Previously this lintel was interpreted as showing Lakshmana cutting off the ear and nose of Surpanakha, the younger sister of Ravana, with Rama and Sita sitting watching. However Dr Uraisri Varasarin has suggested that the giant who is being killed was unlikely to be Ravana's younger sister as it looks much more like a man. Instead Dr Uraisri has suggested that the carving probably represents Rama killing Viradha. If this is the case then Rama appears twice in the same scene - killing Viradha in one part and sitting with Sita in the other part (no-one other than Rama could be with her so intimately as Sita is shown sitting on his lap). Carvings with similar characteristics have been found at Banteay Srei. Not only does it correspond to the known legend but it incorporates a half-hidden representation of a bull with its legs tied-up in the air and a simha (between Krishna's legs). Bruno Dagens argues that these must represent the bull Arishta and the simha which were instructed by Kamsa to kill Krishna but were unsuccessful in their attempt. Previous interpretations have neglected to incorporate the presence of these two animals.

This pediment was previously interpreted as a judgment of Brahma Malivaraja, Ravana's uncle. He descended from heaven, represented by the replica of the sanctuary at the top, and appears just below it. Below is Rama on the left and Ravana again on the right. However close inspection shows that underneath the horses hooves may be seen the head of a fallen figure, leading to a different interpretation in which this scene is seen as the last battle and death of Ravana. In this latter interpretation, Ravana appears three times.

The pediment and lintel above the east door of the mandapa. The pediment (opposite) shows a meeting between all the principal gods of the Brahmin faith. From left to right is Brahma on a hamsa, Indra on the elephant Airavata and Vishnu on a Garuda. Above them all (see right) Shiva and Uma are riding on the bull Nandin. Rishis fill the background. It has been suggested that the scene represented in the lintel below with figures in a boat may show Rama and his attendants travelling back to Ayodhya after conquering Ravana at the Battle of Lanka and being blessed by all the deities shown above. This is possible but unconfirmed.

Detail of pediment.

Detail of lintel.

Above *Antefix showing Varuna, guardian of the west, riding on three hamsas. Towards the end of the 11th century and the beginning of the 12th century, a new type of inward-leaning triangular antefix was introduced and was used in conjunction with roofs which had miniature porches and pediments on each level. The slight inward inclination contributes to the curved effect of the prang as a whole (see over).*
Right *Flame motifs over the mandapa entrance.*

Above *The centre of this lintel depicts a dancing divinity, flanked by smaller dancers, with a row of meditating Buddhas above. As the attributes held by the divinity are unclear, he is impossible to identify but probably represents a Boddhisattva.*

Overleaf *The elegantly proportioned stone prasat of Phimai is constructed from sandstone of excellent quality, and stands in a large open space surrounded by a gallery and gopuras. The gallery and the gopuras are built of red sandstone with the window frames and the doors picked out in white sandstone. The gallery has a solid wall on the outside decorated with false windows with balusters, while the inner wall is pierced with window frames at intervals. The arched roof is carved with tiles and there is a series of finials decorating the ridge. The gallery, although constructed from inferior quality sandstone which has collapsed extensively, provides an excellent colour contrast with the main prasat of golden sandstone and the blue sky above.*

Lintel from the north-west gallery. This unidentified scene shows the protagonists in Baphuon style dress, but the presence of a row of hamsas below suggests that the scene is taking place in heaven.

The prang seen through one of the massively framed windows of the surrounding gallery.

The doorway linking the side room with the central room of the eastern gopura. Inside the gopuras are rows of square pillars which provide support for the roof, which in all cases, however, was never constructed. The pillars are extremely large but have not received any carving and the sides and corners are buttressed to the walls in order to increase their strength.

Inside the eastern gopura with its almost fully developed 12th century form. Gopuras developed from very simple rectangles into chambered halls which were almost buildings in their own right. Because of their greater size columns became necessary to support the roof.

Above *The prang seen through a window of the eastern gopura.*

Opposite *The eastern gopura from the outside.*

Above
Carved lintel with six standing Buddhas, in the attitude of Vitarka Mudra, found in the vicinity of Phimai.
This lintel is one of three or four which show standing Buddhas in this position, with both hands held up with thumb and forefinger lightly touching (the Vitarka Mudra) and they show the influence of Dvaravati art in this region. Nevertheless the style of the lower part of the Buddha's robe is similar to garments worn by women in the Baphuon period, characterised by a long central fold with fish-tail end hanging down in front and the wearing of a belt. However it would seem that the carving of the Buddhas was unfinished as the belt has no decorative carving and the necklaces have merely been outlined. The fact that the Buddhas are clothed in a manner similar to women, something forbidden under the disciplinary rules, suggests that a particular sect existed in this area. The carving of the robe shows a deliberate attempt by the craftsman to convey its lightweight quality.

Below
Half of a lintel showing a simha with garland, probably found in the vicinity of Phimai. What is interesting is that the simha plays the dominant role in this carving, being placed in the middle and having a size which fills the depth of the lintel. He is seated in a squatting position and grasps the garland, which would have emerged on both sides, firmly in his mouth while also holding onto it with his claws. Note that in the top quarter of the lintel above the garland may be observed an upturned flower pendant. This feature of an upturned flower pendant appearing in conjunction with richly carved floral motifs is noticeable in virtually every lintel from Phimai. Another characteristic is the extremely deep carving of the swirling foliate motifs.

Above
This lintel still employs a Baphuon narrative technique in which large figures fill the whole, although the lintel probably dates to the beginning of the Angkor Wat period. It depicts the ancient Indian Ashvamedha ceremony in which the King releases the best horse in the kingdom to wander free for one year. During this time a band of soldiers follows the horse discreetly. Any town visited by the horse had to receive it in an appropriate manner to show their loyalty to the King; if not the town would be crushed by the soldiers. On the horse's return to the capital, a ceremony presented the horse to the gods. In the Ramayana, Rama himself carried out such a ceremony on his return to Ayodhya. Here, the head of the procession is shown pouring water on to the hands of the principal Brahmin, with the horse behind.

Below
The multi-panel design of this broken lintel is quite unusual in that the various elements are clearly separated. The row of seated Buddhas at the top left indicates its Mahayanist iconography. A divinity with two consorts occupies the central panel (at the right of this fragment), while the row of apsaras and the frieze of hamsas indicate the celestial location.

Overleaf
A general view of Phimai taken from the west.

PRASAT PHNOM RUNG

ปราสาทพนมรุ้ง

Opposite
Within the enclosure the remains of brick towers with a surviving sandstone door frame, can be confidently dated to the 10th century. The central sanctuary behind, as with most of the other surviving structures, is from the late 12th century.

Above
Aerial view from the north shows the processional staircase at left rising to the main enclosure.

The inscriptions of Prasat Phnom Rung offer a unique insight into the nature of Khmer rule in Northeast Thailand between the 10th and 13th centuries AD. They record the family history of Narendraditya and his son, Hiranya, making it clear that they ruled autonomously, not as vassals to the king at Angkor. Some of this history is depicted on the narrative reliefs adorning the main sanctuary. If, as they appear to, these reliefs do relate to Narendraditya's life, they represent the earliest portraiture and carving of historical scenes in Khmer art.

Let us begin with the setting, for the name 'Phnom Rung' refers to the ancient volcano upon which the temple sits. Phnom Rung hill rises over 350 metres above the surrounding plain. On a fine day, one can gaze across the floodplain below. The eye is first caught by the sparkle of water in the baray or reservoir of the neighbouring temple of Muang Tam, and then by the dark grey foothills of the Dangrek Mountains, the border of Cambodia. The strategic value of the hill-top location of Phnom Rung continues to be appreciated today by the Thai Royal Air Force, who share the crest of the mountain with the ancient temple. In former times, Phnom Rung was midway between the great city of Angkor to the south and Phimai to the northwest. The ruler who controlled the Phnom Rung area most probably also had suzerainity over the fertile floodplain stretching south to Prasat Muang Tam. This powerful fiefdom appears to have been held during one of the most prosperous periods of the region's history, by the family of Narendraditya.

Altogether eleven inscriptions have been found at Phnom Rung. The name 'Phnom Rung' itself appears once on a stele inscribed with a Sanskrit eulogy and several times in the Khmer inscriptions. It is unusual for temples to retain their original Khmer names which here means 'broad mountain'.

The earliest of the inscriptions found at Prasat Phnom Rung is in Sanskrit. It is only four lines, but has been dated to around the 7th or 8th century. This date precedes that of the 9th century usually given to the existing structures within the temple complex. Therefore, the inscription either came from another place such as the neighbouring peak of Phu Angkhan, or belonged to an earlier sanctuary which has now been built over. (This is known to have happened at Phimai, where a brick structure was discovered underlying the stone temple).

Of the other Sanskrit inscriptions, the most important bears the inventory number of K.384. It is also the biggest, measuring about 27 x 53 centimetres. In the early part of this century, Aymonier first noticed the stone in a wat in Nakhon Ratchasima and it was moved to Bangkok by Prince Damrong. Although it was thought to have come from Khao Phnom Rung, this was not confirmed until 1972, when a second piece of the stele was found during Fine Arts Department reconstruction of the temple. This second fragment, matched the first in both size and in its 12th century Sanskrit characters.

The inscription was erected by Narendraditya's son, Hiranya, perhaps to commemorate the founding of new additions to the Saivite monastery at Phnom Rung. It begins with a hymn to Shiva, in particular of the Shiva Mahayogi, supreme patron of all ascetics. Hiranya set up a golden image of his father, and other members of the family presented gifts in his honour. The family were members of the Mahidharapura dynasty who originated in this area. During Narendraditya's lifetime, one of his relatives, King Suryavarman II (1112-1152) ruled from Angkor. Suryavarman naturally used his ties to the Northeast to bring this region under his power. In fact, earlier scholars such as George Cœdès who examined the K.384 stele concluded that it was a hymn to Suryavarman II. However, the work of HRH Princess Maha Chakri Sirindhorn has established that the inscription praises Narendraditya. The importance of the inscription lies in the insight it offers into the independence of the Northeastern governorships which came under the sway of Angkor. Men such as Narendraditya were powerful chiefs who found it advantageous to pay tribute to the wealthy ruler at Angkor.

In the case of Narendraditya, the K.384 inscription records that he assumed suzerainity over the Phnom Rung principality after he had defeated many enemies in the service of King Suryavarman II. These may even have been the campaigns which enabled Suryavarman II to assume the throne, and are depicted on some of the bas-reliefs of the temple complex. Shortly after this, however, Narendraditya became a yogi and guru, retreating from the ceaseless struggle for power into the meditative world of the monastery. This at any rate, is how his son Hiranya recorded events in 1150 AD, when he decided to commemorate his father's history with the setting up of the inscription and golden image.

Hiranya has also set out his own biography, noting that at the age of 15 he completed a grammar course and graduated at 16. By the age of 18, he had proven his prowess as a hunter of elephants, and at 20 had the golden image of his father made. Presumably, these dedications by Hiranya were made to celebrate an addition to the monastery and a bid for control based on deification of his father, and identification of himself with this power. Unfortunately we know nothing more of the family's history, for the K.384 inscription is the last to be erected at Phnom Rung.

Among the other inscriptions, however, are fascinating details of the religious practices of the monastery on Phnom Rung hill. One, with an inventory number of BR.14, is carved on a rounded stone slab almost a metre high, a shape associated with sema stones or bounday markers. The inscription on the stone dates to the 12th century, and refers to a pool called Sri Surya, as well as the setting up of images of the gods. These included a linga, emblem of the god Shiva, and an image of Vishnu.

Free-standing stone sculptures of deities such as Brahma and Shiva's elephant-headed son Ganesha found at Phnom Rung show that worship of a number of Hindu gods spanned several centuries. For example, the statue of Brahma has a cylindrical head-dress covered in pearls, and a pleated sampot which hangs from his belt in a fish-tail pattern. These features allow the piece to be dated stylistically to the 10th century. The statues of Ganesha typically show the god with his trunk curled to his left in order to dip into the small pot containing a favourite sweet offered by his followers. One of these, now in the Mahavirawong Museum in Nakhon Ratchasima, has been dated to the 8th century AD Prei Kmeng style. This conclusion was reached by comparing the style of Ganesha's sampot and belt with statuary from the Cambodian remains at Angkor Borei.

As the earliest remains within the Phnom Rung complex, the bases of two brick sanctuaries, date to the early 10th century, the Ganesha statue may have been brought to the monastery at a later date. On the other hand, it does seem that there was once a third brick structure which has now been built over with the central sandstone temple. Following on from this evidence it seems probable that the mountain top was a place of worship for a variety of sects for several hundred years preceding the construction of the buildings visible today. Earlier structures could well have dated to the 8th century AD; certainly remains on the neighbouring peak of Phu Angkhan date to this period. Whatever the case may be, the important point is the evidence for a highly syncretic blend of devotions by pilgrims and ascetics at Phnom Rung.

Some of the worship appears to have been Tantric influenced, a practice which was more widespread in Khmer areas in Thailand than Cambodia. For instance, one of the Khmer inscriptions lists offerings to the gods, which included salt, rice, goats, pigs, oil, sesame, beans, and rice whisky. This last item may have been used in Tantric ceremonies. Whichever ritual was being celebrated, the rishis or ascetics of the monastery were present to conduct the ceremony. The importance of the religious community at Phnom Rung is evident not only in the scope of the temple complex, but in the proliferation of carvings of ascetics - forming the decoration on pilaster bases, seated in a line across the upper register of lintels, and as the central figure on pediments. The rishis are readily identifiable, with their pointed beards and matted locks arranged in a jatamukuta chignon. They are usually seated with their knees drawn up in a position of meditation although the figure of Shiva as the supreme ascetic on the pediment of the outer eastern gopura, is seated in the position of lalitasana.

The approach to the temple of Phnom Rung, and the precinct of the rishis, however, begins far below the outer gateway. It is not uncommon today to see a group of pilgrims winding their way on foot up the paved highway to Phnom Rung. Since completion of the seventeen year restoration programme of the Fine Arts Department in 1988, thousands of visitors have come to the temple. Many, foreigners and Thais alike, are tourists, come to view the famous monuments, have a good meal from the local

Opposite
The eastern approach to the sanctuary from the 'naga bridge' which can barely be recognised in the foreground.

Above
The same approach after restoration some 70 years later.

foodstalls and open-air restaurants, and perhaps buy a modern stone carving as a souvenir. Others, however, come as pilgrims to participate in the spiritual heritage of the mountain. The Buddhist monastic community which cared for the precinct until it was made a Fine Arts Department Historical Park, recently consecrated a new image of the Buddha for their shrine. Thus, while the ancient temple was Hindu, modern worshippers continue the tradition of merit-making instituted by their ancestors.

The plan of the temple

The lower staircase of Phnom Rung is still partly covered in vegetation, almost half a kilometre down the eastern slope of the hill. These laterite steps lead up to the first of four cruciform platforms which mark the ascent to the eastern entrance. The platform is large, measuring 40 metres from north to south and 30 metres from east to west. The presence of steps below the platform suggests that a pavilion once rose above it, to mark its importance on the way to the summit. This type of layout is found at other Khmer temples such as Wat Phu in Laos, and Preah Vihear to the east of Phnom Rung on the Thai-Cambodian border. Like Phnom Rung, remains of buildings at both Wat Phu and Preah Vihear show that they were places of worship many centuries earlier.

Immediately north of the cruciform platform is a large laterite and sandstone building known as the White Elephant Pavilion or Elephant Stables. This name refers to local tradition rather than historical fact. As it was popularly supposed that Phnom Rung was a king's pavilion and that the king's elephant had to be stabled somewhere, this building was locally-believed - wrongly - to have had this function.

The pavilion faces the platform, with a gallery surrounding a twenty metre long porch on the east, west, and north sides. Roof tiles found around the building show that it was once covered over. The pavilion may date to the late 10th century, but appears to have also been restored during the late 12th century. A gold plaque delicately inscribed with a lotus was found here during reconstruction by the Fine Arts Department. The plaque was probably buried beneath the building at the time of its original consecration.

The processional way, 160 metres long, connects the cruciform platform with the next set of stairs leading up to the temple. The esplanade is paved with blocks of laterite, and bordered with sandstone. On either side are 67 sandstone boundary stones, each over a metre high, and carefully positioned just over four metres apart. The squared bases of these pillars taper into the rounded curve of the lotus in a style typical of the early part of the 12th century.

At the end of the processional way is a second cruciform platform, known as the 'naga bridge'. The 'naga bridge' of Phnom Rung is one of the finest ever carved. Constructed of sandstone, it is raised up about one and a half metres. It can be mounted by staircases on the north and south, as well as the main ascent on the east. Underneath, the platform is supported by small delicately carved sandstone pillars. A large lotus is lightly inscribed on the stone floor of the platform. This, and an unfinished doorstep suggest that the platform was never completed.

The crowning feature of the 'naga bridge' are the five-headed nagas, their bodies forming the balustrades of the terrace, and their richly crowned heads arching up at the corners. The pilgrim standing on the platform confronts the hooded faces directly for they rise up over a metre from the platform balustrade. Unlike the more subterranean nagas which guard the pools at Prasat Muang Tam, the nagas of Phnom Rung seem to rise up from their water abode in all their glory. Their diadems are minutely carved into five layers studded with jewels, which carry down from the crown to adorn their foreheads. Horizontal lines separate the segments of their neck, with the circle of a lotus embellishing the breast of the central creature. The nagas draw back their lips, not in the voracious manner of the kala, but in guardianship and warning to those who cross the 'bridge'. No detail has been forgotten, with even the rear of their bodies carved with hoods, scales, and backbones. Another lotus nestles just below the hood. The style of carving suggests that all were executed at the same time, during the early part of the 12th century.

The 'naga bridges' link the world of man to that of the gods on the summit of the hill. Having crossed over, the pilgrim ascends the final and grandest staircase. Five sets of stairs, each over 13 metres wide, cover the steep slope. At the top is a wide sandstone and laterite terrace, with four square ceremonial pools. Blocks of stone extend to both sides of this terrace, forming the base of the massive platform, over 100 metres in length, upon which the temple buildings are placed. From the south-eastern corner of this terrace the surrounding plain and the Dangrek Mountains can be seen.

One more 'naga bridge' presents itself to the pilgrim before the compound can be entered. Like those below, this also has a cruciform plan, with nagas guarding each corner. However, unlike the lower cruciform terraces, the balustrades on this upper level are formed from the body of the makara, the mythical animal associated with water. The multiple heads of the naga issue forth from the shallowly carved and stylized jaws of the makara. Small squared pillars once more support the platform. Four sandstone steps, with a final stone carved into a lotus shape, lead up to the terrace.

The main sanctuary of Phnom Rung is enclosed by walled galleries. The construction of these once again recalls the monastery function of the complex, for the galleries are not continuous but are divided into cells, perhaps for meditation. The gallery on the main east entry is the most complete. It is made of sandstone, with both the main and secondary gopuras or gateways having square windows. The way that the stone has been carved is similar to the methods used to construct windows in wood, a reminder of the many wooden structures which would have stood within the monastery.

The roof of the eastern gallery is carved in stone to resemble overlapping tiles. A row of prali (finials) decorate the roof peak. Many parts of the roof, and most of the finials were newly carved during the reconstruction, and reassembled with the remaining original pieces to restore the gallery to its former state. The roof is stepped descending from the centre. Thus on each side of the central cruciform gopura there is a room, complete with false window, whose roof is slightly lower. The pattern is repeated again in the next section, but here can be seen not only windows but the secondary gopuras with their decorative pediments, lintels, pilasters and colonettes. Just as the central doorway of some of Bangkok's royal wats are reserved for entry of the King of Thailand, the only persons to pass under the central doorway of Phnom Rung may have been the king and his chief priest.

A double pediment arches over the gopura. The rear pediment rests upon the corbelled roof, presenting an upward thrust that mirrors both the lotus-shaped spire of the inner temple, and the front pediment directly over the doorway. These two pediments offer a fascinating glimpse of the process of carving the temple, for the rear one is unfinished. The bodies of the two nagas which form the smooth lobes of the pediment frame have been emphasized with three incised bands. At each end, the five heads of the naga jut out protectively. However, a glance at the front pediment shows that their crowns are yet to be carved. The outer band of the pediment and the foliate leaves of the front pediment remain smooth in contrast to the rich detail framing that at the front.

The baroque qualities of the front pediment border make the treatment of space in the central composition all the more surprising. At the centre sits Shiva in his role as the supreme ascetic. The trident ornamenting his head forms the peak of the triangle which encloses the composition. Within this area, every available space has been deeply carved, with some of the most fulsome female figures to be found at Phnom Rung. However, the space between the central scene and the frame has been left empty, most unusual in 12th century Khmer bas-reliefs. A final garland may have been intended as a backdrop, as is the case with the pediment of Shiva as Nataraja or Lord of the Dance above the east entry of the main temple. Or, the sense of space may have been an intentional reference to the life of the rishi, and the monastic achievement which Shiva's manifestation as ascetic embodies.

Passing through the portal under the ascetic's gaze and on to the cruciform terrace beyond, the pilgrim meets Shiva once more. He is no longer the monastic patron but creator and destroyer, Lord of the Dance. There are many stories connected with Shiva as dancer, but it is in his cosmic dance that he is depicted at Phnom Rung.

In Hindu legend, Shiva began to dance after addressing the ascetic yogis, a sequence which perhaps explains the succession of images of Shiva seen at Phnom Rung. Shiva's ten arms are fanned out across the width of the pediment, his right arms rising up somewhat more than his left to counterbalance the lift of his left leg. One of his left hands rests gently on the foliage of the arch which frames him.

Below, although sadly damaged, are the figures of Ganesha, Shiva's elephant-headed son, and two female figures one of which probably represents Kareikkal-ammeyar. Although scholars differ in their opinion of the precise manifestation of Shiva Nataraja which the pediment portrays, the feeling of the artisan who carved the face of the god is clear. He has created a beautifully gentle, almost feminine countenance which ranks among the most expressive of the temple's carvings.

The lintel beneath the pediment of Shiva Nataraja shows the god Vishnu, the preserver. This lintel was missing from the temple for many years, having been sold to an American art foundation. Following long negotiations by Thai art historians, the lintel was returned to Thailand in 1988. During this time, it became the focus of a national campaign to restore to Thailand the many illegally exported antiquities which are housed in foreign museums and art galleries. The successful resolution of the controversy coincided with the completion of the seventeen year restoration project of the temple.

Although today's pilgrim may proceed through Shiva and Vishnu's east entry, in former times the inner sanctuary was open only to priest and king. In the case of the main sanctuary of Phnom Rung, there is even some controversy about whether the garbhagrha was ever entered on the east. The reason for this lies in the difference in floor levels between the three parts of the building: the mandapa, the antarala, and the garbhagrha. The mandapa, the easternmost part of the building, would appear to be the principal entrance, for the temple faces in this direction. The entire approach to the sanctuary leads up to the final encounter with the cosmic figures of Shiva and Vishnu above the east doorway of the mandapa. However, the sandstone floor of the mandapa is about a metre below that of the antarala and garbhagrha. No evidence for stairs was found during reconstruction, although the Fine Arts Department has placed steps there now.

Some scholars feel that the mandapa was used for chanting. Others suggest that it may have served as a secondary shrine, perhaps dedicated to a deity other than Shiva. Wood was used to make a ceiling, to close off the high space created by the corbelled tower above.

The garbhagrha may have been entered on the south, the north entrance having a somasutra, a sandstone channel used to drain away water used during ceremonies. The presence of an acestic holding a rosary, an identifying attribute of Shiva as patron of the rishis shows that the southern entry was an important one. Shiva appears elsewhere on the south side on a pediment in the guise of Umamahesvara, with Shiva seated on his bull Nandin, Uma on his knee. Sadly, only traces remain of the figures of Shiva and Uma. Aside from the figure of Shiva on the east side of the temple, it is only on the south that he appears. As the garbhagrha is thought to have contained the linga, phallic symbol of Shiva's creative power, these carvings suggest that the few admitted to this inner sanctum may have entered on the south.

Another indication of the importance of the south facade is a pediment depicting a battlescene, perhaps a record of Narendraditya's campaigns. The figure on the right stands triumphant on his elephant's head, while one of the enemy hangs from the elephant's trunk. Elsewhere on the south side is another scene which may show Narendraditya. On a lintel over the south portico of the garbhagrha, the central character in a line of seated figures, is dressed as a king. Just behind him sits a rishi. The king's left hand is placed upon an offering table as he enacts the ritual. One explanation for the concentration of significant motifs on the southern side is that this is the direction of the capitol at Angkor, in Cambodia. By paying tribute in this fashion, Narendraditya both declares his stature as chief ascetic of the monastery, and acknowledges his tributary links to King Suryavarman II at Angkor. Whatever the explanation, these historical scenes may be some of the earliest executed by Khmer artisans.

The decorative carvings on all sides of the main sanctuary are impressive. These include not only lintels and pediments, but elaborate patterns incised on the mouldings at the base of the buildings, and foliate designs on the pilasters with a variety of figures carved on the bases. Although the patterns are generally similar to those found on contemporary temples elsewhere in Thailand and Cambodia, some of the decorative motifs are unique to Phnom Rung.

For example, small rows of pearls delineate the top register of many of the moulding designs. Another unique scene now thought to represent a fertility ritual, is found on the base of the right pilaster flanking the east door of the mandapa. A young woman stands with her left arm entwined in the spray of foliage which curls up the pediment. With her left arm she reaches down to accept an offering held by a kneeling servant, while a rishi extends his blessing. This scene was once thought to depict the birth of the Buddha, but unlike other Khmer temples, the monastery at Phnom Rung does not appear to have been Buddhist until modern times.

Another unusual carving is seen on the west lintel and pediment of the main sanctuary. Although generally the lintel and pediment illustrate different stories, in this case both contain an episode of the Ramayana. The heroes of the epic, Rama and Lakshmana have been caught by Nagapasa, the serpent noose. They can be seen wrapped in the coils at the base of the lintel. The evil Ravana has ordered Trijata to take Rama's wife Sita, held captive at Ravana's court, to the battlefield. Sita, fearing her husband is dead, cries, but Trijata reassures her by reminding her that their chariot flies through the air, an impossible feat if a widow is aboard. At Phnom Rung, Sita's chariot fills the pediment above the now badly damaged lintel of Rama and Lakshmana. Monkeys hold the chariot aloft, Sita enclosed in the center. The vehicle is shaped like the main tower of Phnom Rung, complete with Shiva's trident at the summit. A similar scene is found at Prasat Phimai. These are but a few examples of the carvings which embellish much of the exterior of the temple. Like the outer gallery, the roofs of the mandapa, the antarala and the garbhagrha have different levels. Triple porticoes extend from several of the entrances, each adorned with lintels, pediments, and the ubiquitous nagas. In the case of the core of the sanctuary, the garbhagrha, this pediment-lintel combination is repeated further. Above the third pediment, which is carved flush against the wall of the garbhagrha tower, are three sets of lintels and pediments. They are slightly different from those over the porticoes, being more rectangular than the flamboyant outer arches. Numerous antefixes complete the ascending levels of the tower. Naga antefixes are

Opposite
The eastern gopura, naga terrace and pond. There are three entrances to the prasat on the eastern side: the entrance for the most important visitors through the central doorway aligned on the main axis of the site passing through the eastern gopura, and two entrances for less important personages through the gallery on either side of the gopura. The gopura is cruciform in plan and roofed with stone tiles decorated with a row of prali. In front is the final 'naga bridge' and balustrade whose terrace is also cruciform in plan. Originally this terrace was covered with a wooden roof as can be deduced from the holes which remain to this day and would have held the roof supports. The architect then seems to have changed his mind and enlarged the wings of the terrace to incorporate a naga balustrade. The balustrade is formed by the naga's body, supported on short pillars, turning corners to follow the outline of the terrace and terminating in rearing naga heads as at Angkor Wat. In front of the terrace on either side of the path are four small ponds which may symbolize the four sacred rivers of the Indian subcontinent.

placed on the corners but directional gods and guardian figures have been placed along the sides. Each level is proportionally smaller, so that the tower curves in smoothly in the shape of a lotus bud. The kalasa, or vase of plenty, marks the summit. During the time of Narendraditya, the three-points of Shiva's trident may have reached even higher.

The tower of the garbhagrha is the only one remaining today, although several of the other sanctuaries within the walls may once have had superstructures. The oldest of these buildings are the remains of the 10th century brick prasats found in the north-east sector of the courtyard. This dating is derived from a sandstone colonette found near the brick sanctuary facing east. There may have once been a third brick building destroyed during later construction, for many Khmer temples built at this time did consist of a row of three brick cells on a platform. The structures are badly damaged, but their plan is clear, with one facing east and the other south. This suggests the possibility of a dual directionality for the main sanctuary, following a pre-existing layout.

Another building in the courtyard which may have had a tower is known as Prang Noi or 'little tower'. The sanctuary faces east, with false doors on the other three sides. It is mounted on a laterite base, and rather unusually, is lined with laterite blocks. Scholars differ in their opinions about the superstructure of the building. Although it was previously thought that the building may have had a brick tower, as may Prasat Ban Phluang in Surin province, little evidence was found for such a superstructure during excavation, and it is more likely that the sanctuary remained unfinished. Motifs on lintels on the east and south sides of Prang Noi have been dated to the late 10th and early 11th Khleang and Baphuon periods. Thus, like the brick temples, Prang Noi may have stood within the compound before the main sanctuary was built.

The wall which surrounds the inner courtyard also appears to have been erected in several phases. The eastern, western and southern galleries are constructed of sandstone, the entire enclosure measuring some 66 x 88 metres. They are over five metres wide, but do not form a continuous walkway. Rather each section is divided into rooms. During reconstruction, artefacts found in some of these rooms suggest that they may have been used for ritual or meditation. The north gallery differs from the others, being constructed of laterite. It is possible that it dates to the end of the 12th century, a period of Khmer architecture which saw a great increase in the use of laterite.

Above and opposite
Naga balustrade, east entrance gopura.

The eastern pediment from the eastern gopura is one of the most important. In the middle of the upper portion is the figure of a man with the appearance of a Hindu yogi seated in the lalitasana position. His right hand is raised level with his chest and the points of his finger and thumb are touching to form a circle, while his left hand rests on his lap. Girls surround the yogi on all sides. His hair style is similar to that of the dancing Shiva on the eastern pediment of the mandapa, and it has been suggested that this carving represents Shiva in the form of the supreme ascetic. In addition, a further meaning might relate to Prince Narendraditya, the father of Prince Hiranya, who caused Phnom Rung to be built. The Sanskrit inscription found at the site and translated by HRH Princess Maha Chakri Sirindhorn contains passages comparing or even equating Narendraditya with Shiva and supports this theory.

Lintel from the eastern entrance of the eastern gopura showing a divinity sitting on the head of a kala who is holding two simhas. While the pediment above the lintel (opposite) is in Angkor Wat style, here the forms and arrangement are in Baphuon style.

This statue of Ganesha in the 8th century Prei Kmeng style may have been brought here from elsewhere. In any event, it is the oldest artefact found at Phnom Rung. Ganesha has two arms and his trunk is picking up something from the dish held in his left hand. The date of the piece can be established by comparing the style of his belt with that from a Ganesha statue at Angkor Borei. (Mahavirawong Museum, Khorat)

Statue of Brahmi, Koh Ker style, 1st half of the 10th century. Brahmi is one of the Sapta Matrikas or Seven Divine Mothers who include: Brahmi, Maheswari, Vaishnavi, Kaumari, Indrani,Varahi and Chamundi. This seems to be the only statue of Brahmi found in Thailand. She sits with one knee raised and her hands folded in prayer. Her pleated sarong has a border and is folded below her stomach in the Koh Ker manner. Although iconographically correct, the execution of the piece is provencial.(Mahavirawong Museum, Khorat)

This is a fine statue of Brahma although the feet and lower arms have broken off and disappeared. His face, hair style and sampot dates the statue to the 10th century. (Mahivirawong Museum, Khorat)

The pediment above the eastern gallery entrance shows a scene from the Ramayana, although it is difficult to determine the precise events. It certainly depicts a battle between the yakshas in the centre of the carving and the monkey troops who are grabbing and biting them. At the top a monkey leader holds aloft a weapon about to strike a yaksha. This pediment shows the characteristic Angkor Wat desire to fill the available space with as many bodies as possible in many different positions.

Opposite
The corner of the south-eastern gallery is marked by a blind door surmounted by an unfinished lintel echoing the kala-simha theme over the main entrance.

Overleaf
Phnom Rung seen from the south-west.
In the southern courtyard can be seen two buildings which date from a different period to the 12th century main prang. In the foreground may be seen the lesser prang (Prang Noi) which is a small sandstone prang built in the 11th century in the Baphuon style. In fact the outside is constructed of sandstone while the inside is laterite. The superstructure has all collapsed and disappeared and it is likely that the sandstone would have been used to build something else and therefore no traces have been found during restoration. This small prang has an entrance on the east while the other three sides have false doors. The entrance is not adorned with a porch of any kind. Professor Jean Boisselier has stated that the practice of carving a pediment on a rectangular surface as seen here is one that did not occur in Cambodia, where the pediment would be constructed in a curved shape as seen in the main prang. Accordingly it may be considered as a method peculiar to this part of the country.
The other building is a rectangular laterite structure which faces west and is situated in the right of the photograph. It is a 'library' which was added to the site during the Bayon period in the 13th century.

The lintel over the east entrance to the Prang Noi is in a mixture of the Khleang and Baphuon styles. The vertical floral pendants at both quarters of the lintel are Khleang, while the divinity seated over the kala face is typical of the Baphuon period.

The eastern lintel from the mandapa showing Vishnu Anantasayin is possibly the best known in all Thailand due to the fame it acquired when it was discovered to have been stolen and sold to the Art Institute of Chicago. Before Phnom Rung's restoration, the lintel lay on the ground in front of the doorway (see oppposite). It shows Vishnu reclining on the back of the naga king in the milky ocean, sleeping between two kalpas. Although the curling foliage is in the Baphuon style, Vishnu and Lakshmi's apparel is characteristic of the Angkor Wat period. Vishnu sleeps on a many-headed naga adorned with head-dresses and the naga is in turn lying on a dragon. These characteristics are typical of true Angkor Wat style. The right-hand side of the lintel carries the unusual motif of two finely carved parrots below a kala (see overleaf).

Dancing Shiva from the eastern mandapa pediment.
The pediment above the Vishnu lintel at the east entrance to the mandapa is as at Phimai a representation of Dancing Shiva in true early Angkor Wat style. The actual frame of the pediment is plain except for a single four-petalled flower carved at various intervals, while the outer and inner parts have several bands of carving which echo the curving outline of the frame. The dating may also be ascertained by Shiva's apparel such as his head-dress, necklace and sampot and the way in which the hair is pulled up and then allowed to flow out in two pigtails. While Shiva with 10 arms is found both in northern and southern India, this particular representation shows more southern influence in the lightly carved framing pattern above his head and behind his body which is reminiscent of the curving flame-like patterns of Tamil art.

A detail from the northern pediment of the mandapa, early Ankor Wat style. This carving illustrates one of the battle scenes from the Ramayana. Here the monkey troops are flying down from the sky to attack the asuras. Some are holding branches of wood in their hands instead of weapons. Above a large flock of birds is also descending. All in all, this is an extremely fine carving, full of movement.

Pediment from the southern entrance of the mandapa showing Umamahesvara. Although substantial parts of the carving are missing, including the figures of Shiva and Uma, the bull Nandin is finely carved in very deep relief. The tiered pediments together with the flame motifs contribute to the height and presence of the entrance.

The mandapa from the north-east, before and after restoration. The porches of the mandapa give it a cruciform plan. From the outside the height of the mandapa and the stepped pediments produce a two-storey effect. The antarala connecting the mandapa to the prang has entrance doors on the north and south in contrast to Phimai which only has false windows.

Interior lintel over the doorway leading from the mandapa and antarala to the main prang. The presence of the five rishis, their palms together in salutation seated under five arches, confirms that this site was dedicated to the Shiva cult. Their depiction was very popular in the 12th century until the 13th century, as were similar lintels with five Buddha images.

Lotus flowers from the door sill of the eastern entrance to the mandapa. Their presence proves that this entrance was purely symbolic as the lotus flowers could not be stepped on.

Above the northern entrance to the antarala is a rather worn pediment showing a scene from the Ramayana in which Sita is being abducted by Ravana, at left. Rama is shown killing Marica with Lakshmana seated by Rama. Above Ravana with his captive is pursued by Satayu, mythical bird and friend of Rama and Sita, and below at left carrying her away. Unusual in Khmer art is the introduction of an erotic element into the scene - that of two quite large monkeys copulating in the tree below the horse's hooves.

Left: *Antefix from the northern face of the main prang showing Kubera, the deity who guards the northern direction. He is seated on a simha, whose back is so long that he closely resembles the dragon from the lintel carved with the reclining Vishnu. On the cornice of the prang on all four directions are antefixes carved with the deity responsible for that particular direction: Indra on the east, Yama on the south, Varuna on the west and Kubera on the north.*

Right: *Carving of a simha at the base of one of the pilasters framing the northern doorway of the prang.*

Pediment from west entrance of the prang showing a scene from the Ramayana in which Sita is carried on the backs of monkeys in a chariot which is a miniature replica of the temple.

This frieze from the sanctuary base of the main prang is carved from pink sandstone and composed of large diamond-shaped flower clusters alternating with small four-petalled flowers and luxuriant curling foliage. This type of decorative carving was popular on the bases of buildings. Good examples of such carving are found at Phimai and Phnom Rung. Later such patterns were to be an important influence for Thai-style designs during the Ayutthaya period.

Nagas from the corners of the pediments of the main prang. The nagas from the end of pediment frames at Phnom Rung show the true characteristics of the early Angkor Wat style. Pediment frames are plain but carved and scored with many parallel bands following the line of the pediment itself both on the inner and outer edges. Small four-petalled flowers also decorate the frames and most importantly the kalas spewing forth nagas, absent from pediments in the 11th century, reappear in a new guise resembling makaras. The nagas at the ends of the pediments, which in the Baphuon period were either bald-headed or at the end of that period had small auras intertwined with leaves as at Phimai, have now given way to nagas with large crowns.

For a long time it was believed that this style of head-dress originated at Prasat Beng Mealea. However close comparison of the head-dress details of that site and Phnom Rung reveal certain differences. The head-dresses of the Beng Mealea nagas have the same type of carving as those of the deities but with more rows, whereas the head-dresses of the Phnom Rung nagas have rows of tiny leaves one on top of the other with the outer edges of the head-dresses pointing up slightly. Now it is known that Prasat Beng Mealea post-dated Angkor Wat but preceded the Bayon. Thus the theory regarding the naga head-dresses has had to be revised. It is now believed that head-dresses in the Phnom Rung style originated in the Northeast of Thailand, perhaps at Prasat Kamphaeng Yai to be further developed at Phnom Rung.

Left *Antefix at cornice level on the southern face of the prang, showing Yama, guardian of the south, seated on a buffalo.*

Centre *Inclined antefixes on the cornice featuring nagas and dikpalakas. The incline is deliberate to reinforce the inward-curving profile of the prang.*

Right *Pediment over the eastern entrance to the main prang depicting a scene from the story of Krishna Govardhana.*

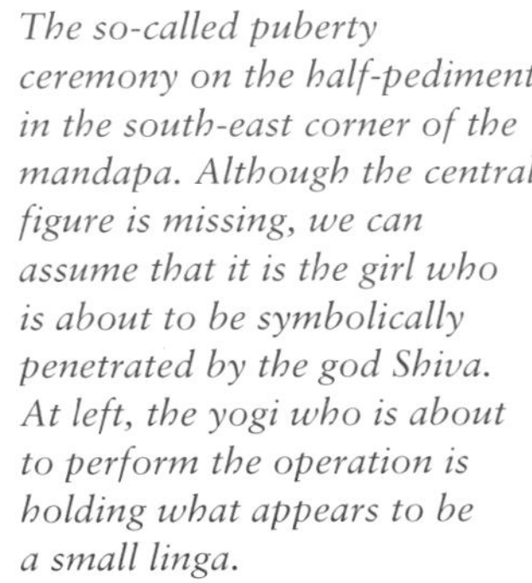

The so-called puberty ceremony on the half-pediment in the south-east corner of the mandapa. Although the central figure is missing, we can assume that it is the girl who is about to be symbolically penetrated by the god Shiva. At left, the yogi who is about to perform the operation is holding what appears to be a small linga.

The pediment over the south entrance to the sanctuary. The poor condition of the scene makes it difficult to decipher but the conch shell visible in the upper left hand of the central four-armed figure identifies the god as Vishnu.

A scene from the Ramayana is illustrated in the upper pediment over the southern entrance to the mandapa. Rama and his brother, Lakshmana are fighting with the giant, Viradha, in the forest.

The sanctuary tower taken from the north-west corner.

PRANG KU SUAN TAENG

กู่สวนแตง

Prang Ku Suan Taeng is situated in the Puthai Song district of Buriram and dates to the mid-12th century. All three brick prangs stand on a low laterite base, facing east in a row along a north-south axis. The middle tower seen here most prominently is the highest and also differs in various details from the two side towers. It is the only one that includes a porch and a façade with a false door. The other two merely have brick side walls which protrude slightly and are otherwise quite plain.

Inside the main prang is a corbelled vault which is still in an excellent state of preservation. Part of the vaulting remains in the northern prang, while the southern prang on the left side of the picture has collapsed completely.

To the east of the three prangs, de Lajonquière noted in the course of his 1904-05 survey the presence of two other laterite buildings, one to the north and one to the south of the central axis in the normal position for 'libraries' although their entrances on the eastern side are unusual for such buildings. In addition, he noted that the buildings were some 800 metres to the east of the site. Furthermore there was also a large pond which may have been a baray. Today the features noted by de Lajonquière have completely disappeared although parts of the earth-rammed walkway to the pond can still be distinguished.

Opposite
The three prangs from the south-east.
Above
The false western door of the central prang in which the door frame and central strip are made of sandstone, while the door panels are built of brick with an absence of the customary moulding. The sandstone slab above functional lintel the acts as a base for the pediment. In previous periods, the decorative lintel was hooked into the functional lintel; but here at Ku Suan Taeng, the decorative lintel was supported by colonettes, and this is the earliest example of this technique found in Thailand.

Right
Lintel from above the eastern doorway of the southern prang. The image of Indra on his elephant Airavata as guardian of the eastern doorway first appeared on Khmer lintels in the time of Sambor Prei Kuk (c.600-650 AD) and continued to remain popular during the whole Khmer period. Stylistically this lintel is completely different from the other two (below and below right). While the general composition of this lintel is Baphuon in style, the details of execution greatly resemble to the Reclining Vishnu Lintel (opposite above). They could almost be carved by the same artist. As the Reclining Vishnu lintel dates to no earlier than the mid-12th century, then this lintel is probably of similar date. (Khon Kaen Museum)

Below
This lintel illustrating Vishnu incarnated as a dwarf (Vamanavatara) is in true Angkor Wat style. All the available space is filled with people and animals, while the head-dresses, ornaments and sampots are clearly from that period. Vishnu appears twice: in the middle part of the lintel where he steps over the ocean and on the extreme right where he is subduing King Bali. (Phimai Museum)

Opposite Above
Lintel above the eastern doorway of the northern prang. This lintel represents a late example of an ever-popular theme -Reclining Vishnu. Its transitional quality is evidenced by the naga's greatly diminished role before its complete disappearance during the Bayon period. The women's hairstyles and the poses of the flying deities are similar to the previously described, suggesting that all were carved by the same group of artists. (Bangkok Museum)

Below left
Lintel above the false door on the western side of the main prang showing The Churning of the Sea of Milk.
This subject is one of the most popular in the whole Khmer iconography, although it occurs more frequently at Angkor than in Thailand.
The details of this episode are well illustrated despite the fact that the heads of the demons and gods have been hacked away. From traces of stone left from the group at the tail of the naga it seems that their hair was loose (as was common for demons) and they did not wear earrings (look at the last person near the naga's tail), while the group at the head of the naga have pointed earrings normally worn by divinities. This leads us to believe that the artists may have misinterpreted the narrative in reversing the positions normally talcen by the divinities and demons. The local love of nature can be seen in the portrayal of numerous animals between the legs of the various deities and demons. Round flowers with sharp leaves pointing towards the top of the lintel can be seen throughout.
While the main elements of the composition are Baphuon in style, the details show the influence of Angkor Wat. (Phimai Museum)

PRASAT TA MUEN TOCH

ปราสาทตาเมือนโต๊ด

Opposite
Photographed from the south-west.

Above
The roots and branches of a strangler fig enclose and support the sandstone blocks.

Situated a few hundred metres from the older prasat of Ta Muen Tom in the Ta Muen district of Surin province, this site in the Bayon style dates from the reign of Jayavarman VII. From an inscription found here it is known that Prasat Ta Muen Toch is the chapel of a hospital. The inscription praises the Lord Buddha and Bhaisajyaguru and states that King Jayavarman VII, the son of Dharnindravarman, was the builder of this hospital for the benefit of the local population. In addition it details the doctors and the nurses, who were both male and female, the various ceremonial articles and the medicines dispensed. Additional information can be gleaned from the Ta Prohm inscription at Angkor (inscribed in the year AD 1186 and translated by George Cœdès) in which it was stated that 102 hospitals such as this one were built in the various towns by royal command throughout the kingdom. The merit accruing from such buildings would pass to the mother of Jayavarman VII and Jayavarman himself with the added proviso that he might become a Buddha in his next life. Ta Muen Toch is the hospital which is nearest to the current Thai-Cambodian border and in the thirteenth century it would have been the first hospital encountered by travellers on the road from Angkor and lower Cambodia through the pass in the Dangrek Mountains to Phnom Rung and Phimai. The hospitals would seem to have been built from less durable materials than other structures and all that remains today are the chapels.

This hospital chapel differs from others such as Kamphaeng Noi in that the body of the prang, as well as the entrance, the pediment and the top of the roof were constructed of sandstone. Other hospitals found in Thailand have laterite chapels with only the ornamental pillars, the door frames and the top of the prang being sandstone.

PRASAT TA MUEN & PRASAT BAN BU

ปราสาทตาเมือนและบ้านบุ

Opposite
The 'house with fire' of Ta Muen, 100 metres north of Ta Muen Toch.

Carved rosette, Ban Bu.

The Preah Khan inscription from Angkor describes how Jayavarman VII had 121 'houses with fire' built along the major roads of his empire. On the road from the capital to Vimaya (Phimai) were constructed 17 such buildings. Research indicates that both Ta Muen and Ban Bu were chapels to resting places. Architecturally they can be related to that at Prasat Preah Khan 173 in Cambodia, having chapels with very long entrances and windows only on the southern side. Only the door frames, the lintels, the crown of the towers and the roof ornaments are sandstone, the rest being built from laterite.

At Ban Bu, which is not so well-preserved as Ta Muen, we can see that the builders have incorporated material from other sites. The door frames are carved with floral motifs and thus must have been taken from some other prasat, where they probably formed part of the wall decoration. An alternative local name for Ta Muen is Prasat Bay Kream which in Khmer means 'laterite sanctuary'.

The western entrance of Ban Bu.

PRASAT KAMPHAENG NOI

ปราสาทกำแพงน้อย

Opposite
The crudely built prang seen from the north-west corner of the enclosure.

Above
The collapsed east entrance gopura seen from inside the enclosure.

The enclosure of Kamphaeng Noi in Uthumphon Phisai district of Sisaket province is on a slight rise, surrounded by a modern monastery. Despite this longterm use, the site preserves much of its original plan, including a reservoir or baray to the east of the temple, and a crumbling laterite annex. A great deal of public building was carried out during the reign of Jayavarman VII. Many of the structures were hastily built and were rather poor technically. Accordingly, many have collapsed and it is difficult to find one in good condition. The builders made use of stone and lintels from existing stuctures and the lintels found here have been reused from an earlier ruined Baphuon prasat, the location of which is still unknown. Such a lintel can be seen in the gopura illustrated.

An outer wall of laterite surrounds an area of about 20 by 35 metres. The wall is pierced only on the east by a cruciform gopura made of laterite and sandstone. Although much of the gate has fallen down, the face of a kala on the lintel over the doorway still guards the entry. Holes which can still be seen in many of the blocks allowed them to be pegged and tied for lifting into position.

The central laterite tower, representing the chapel of the 13th century hospital, is a redented square, each side measuring about five metres. On the east is a square porch, about three metres long. The three other sides of the building have false doors. Hospitals, such as this, have identical ground plans and differ only in their relative sizes. The size of the structure probably corresponded to the size of the local community. Generally the east-facing prang would contain an image of Buddha Bhaisajyaguru and Vajradhara. In the south-east corner of the enclosure would be situated a 'library' facing west. The walls would have one gopura on the eastern side. On the north-east side outside the wall would be a small, square pond whose laterite rim would be stepped.

PRASAT MUANG SINGH

ปราสาทเมืองสิงห์

Opposite
The eastern gopura from the south-east corner of the enclosure. If we compare the picture of this gopura before and after restoration one can see that extensive and unacceptable changes have taken place. It is much to be regretted that what could have been an example of Khmer art carried out farthest from the centre by folk craftsmen has been reconstructed before a thorough study had been made. The historical value of the site has thus been greatly diminished.

Prasat Muang Singh, 'the sanctuary tower of the city of the lion', is located in Kanchanaburi province in the western part of Thailand, close to the Burmese border. The architecture does not pose a problem in dating the Bayon style temple, namely to the reign of Jayavarman VII, 13th century AD. In the Preah Khan inscription of Jayavarman VII mention is made of the various cities to which were sent the statue of Jayabuddhamahanartha. Among these towns are many which we can believe were in Thailand such as Rajapura or Rajburi, Ravapura or Lopburi, Vajrabura or Petchaburi and Srijayasimhapura which is likely to be Muang Singh.

This prasat was discovered during the time of King Chulalongkorn (1868-1910) and registered with the Fine Arts Department since 1935, but a full excavation and restoration has only been carried out recently. The excavations have revealed that laterite was the chief construction material which is typical of the Bayon style overall and the quarries which supplied the laterite have been located not far to the east of the temple. What is unusual is that sandstone has not been used for the door frames, lintels and pediments. Instead where decoration was required stucco has been used, a technique popular in the area of the Chao Phraya basin in the earlier Dvaravati period.

Like Prasat Ta Muen Thom, the location of Muang Singh was strategic. Commanding a vital outpost for the Angkorean king Jayavarman VII (1181-1218), the ruler of Muang Singh controlled a critical portion of the empire. The geographical conquest in the late 12th and early 13th centuries was always affirmed with the establishment of a new temple. Another as-yet unexcavated Khmer sanctuary known as Muang Krut or 'city of the Garuda' is located a few kilometres east of Muang Singh. As the remains in this area are more fully documented in coming years, the image of Muang Singh as a lonely outpost may change to show it as one of a number of prosperous trading centres of the late 12th century.

At Muang Singh, as at earlier large sites, both the temple and the outer limits of the city replicate the cosmos. The plan of the outer rectangular enclosure, the city limits, is somewhat irregular. Measuring about 800 by 1400 metres, it is situated on the banks of the Kwai Noi River. The southern border, rather than completing a perfect rectangle, has a spur on its southern side in order to follow the course of the river. The outer barrier is built of laterite on top of an earthen rampart. Seven more encircling

The site before reconstruction showing the main prang which had entrances on all four sides. Photo: Smitthi Siribhadra.

Detail of the laterite construction, showing traces of stucco work.

Some 30 metres west from this site, is another group of buildings whose structure and interrelationship is very complicated. And it is to be regretted that the restoration has not been fully carried out and the two groups of buildings cannot be studied as a whole.

moats and earthen ramparts on the north, east and west of the temple complete the replication of the celestial universe. The survival of these multiple city enclosures is rare. They are also invaluable in helping to recreate a sense of the Khmer temple as centre of a much larger fortified city.

The rectangular wall of the temple is also laterite. Its enclosure is about one-tenth of that of the city, measuring about 81 by 104 metres. Within this is another, smaller rectangle, that of the galleries. The first indication of the Mahayana Buddhist affiliation of the complex is seen on the inside of the north gallery wall, in the form of the compassionate Bodhisattva, Avalokitesvara carved into the laterite face. The quarries which supplied the laterite for the complex have been located, not far to the east of the temple. The rough finish of the laterite blocks provided a good base for the application of stucco, which once covered the exterior of the temple. The many pieces of stucco recovered during the Fine Arts Department's reconstructions offer a glimpse of the temple as it was during the time of Jayavarman VII. The heads in particular also indicate a sequence of Mon Dvaravati, Khmer Bayon, and Thai influences on the styles of decoration.

In the absence of inscriptions, it has been statues recovered during excavations which have provided the best means of dating the temple. Many portray Mahayana figures such as Avalokitesvara and Prajñaparamita. Avalokitesvara is one of the most frequently seen Bodhisattvas of Mahayana Buddhism. He is one of the five jinas created by the Adi-Buddha. These jinas or 'victorious ones' are each associated with directions, with the jina of the west being Amitabha. If evoked, Amitabha, has the power to cause a person to be born in his next life in paradise, thereby assuring that Buddhahood will be attained in the next existence.

All the jinas are also associated with multiple emmanations of Bodhisattvas and other deities. The most important emanation of Amitabha is Avalokitesvara, known as the compassionate Bodhisattva. It is in part from Avalokitesvara that the visible universe is created; his compassionate aspect derives from the way in which he has delayed his own attainment of Buddhahood to assist all humans in reaching enlightenment.

Of the various attributes associated with Avalokitesvara, two can still be seen on one of the statues of the Bodhisattva recovered from Muang Singh. In this case, Avalokitesvara is shown as Lokesvara or 'lord of the world' holding a book, flask, lotus and rosary. The statue still holds all but the last. A small seated figure of Amitabha can be seen on the front of his cylindrical chignon. The style of the short pleated skirt with its wide belt and anchor-shaped drape, is typical of the late 12th and early 13th centuries. The deity's broad features closely resemble those of the Bayon's face towers, which are believed to represent King Jayavarman VII as Lokesvara.

The central enclosure from the top of the south-west corner of the gallery. The base of the prang still shows remnants of the stucco work which once covered the entire structure.

*Irradiating Lokesvara,
Bayon style, 13th century.
(National Museum, Bangkok)*

*Lokesvara, provincial style,
mid-13th century.
(National Museum, Bangkok)*

These two stone sculptures of Lokesvara were both found in the vicinity. The eight-arm example at left is of classic Bayon style and was either brought from Cambodia or carved by an experienced Khmer craftsman, while the four-armed figure on the ritht is an attempt by a local sculptor to emulate the Khmer style. The eight-armed 161 cm figure is shown in the form known as irradiating, so called from the small figures of the Amitabha Buddha carved all over his torso, arms, forehead, ankles and even his toes. On the chest and around the waist are depicted figures of an unidentified diety of Mahayana Buddhism. The second more crudely proportioned statue carved by a local craftsman represents a four-armed Lokesvara, holding his usual attributes of a flask, lotus and book. As in the Khmer statue a small seated figure of Amitabha Buddha can be seen on the front of his cylindrical chignon, which the local sculptor has incorrectly shown in splayed out fashion.

ITINERARIES

With the exception of Muang Singh, which can be visited on a day trip by road from Bangkok, all of the Khmer sanctuaries featured in this book are on the Khorat Plateau, for which the gateway city is Nakhon Ratchasima, normally referred to as Khorat. As the closest city to the largest sanctuary, Phimai, and within easy driving distance of Phnom Rung and Muang Tam, Khorat is the most popular base for a visit, at least for one or two nights.

An itinerary for visiting the Khmer sanctuaries of the Northeast depends on the number of temples to be included and on the transport available. The ideal is a private car with driver, using one or more of the provincial capitals as overnight stops. Self-drive cars can be hired in Bangkok, and the driving time to Khorat is approximately four hours, although the actual exit from and re-entry to Bangkok can hardly be described as pleasant. Hiring a car with driver removes much of the strain of negotiating the capital's horrendous traffic and solves some of the problems in finding the less well-visited sanctuaries. The alternative to driving all the way from Bangkok up onto the Khorat Plateau is to go directly to Khorat by air, rail or express air-conditioned bus, and hire transport from there.

The key sites to visit and which should on no account be missed, are Phimai and its museum, Phnom Rung and nearby Muang Tam. Then, because they are close to or on the routes between these three major sancuaries, Phnom Wan, Muang Khaek, Non Ku, and the Si Khiu quarry can be added easily as short stops. This makes up the first recommended itinerary, needing one overnight stop in Khorat. The details are given below, and it is shown on the map on page 334.

Developing this short itinerary into a fuller one makes it possible to visit sites further east. One factor that would affect a longer ininerary is the possibility of access to Preah Vihear. Without a doubt, this is one of the most important of all Khmer sanctuaries, and its spectacular location is unique. Unfortunately, its location with regard to the national frontier is also unique, being in Cambodia but only reachable practically from the Thai side. Over much of the past few decades it has to all intents been out of bounds to visitors, but political circumstances change, and as of the time of writing access is possible. If it continues to be, this should strongly influence any itinerary; Preah Vihear alone is worth the long journey from Bangkok.

If Preah Vihear cannot be visited, the second itinerary needing two overnight stops includes a selection of sites with different appeals. Ban Phluang is a quiet, well-maintained and beautifully restored single-cell sanctuary, while Ta Muen Thom and the associated Ta Muen Toch and Ta Muen are very evocative sites in their forest locations. Sikhoraphum is a small jewel on the edge of a small village, while Kamphaeng Yai is a surprisingly substantial sanctuary tucked away just a minute from the road among houses and a modern wat near Sisaket. Surin, a much smaller provincial capital than Khorat, has the best facilities for a second overnight stop. If Preah Vihear cannot be visited, the two-night itinerary will take in most of the other temples.

Visiting any of these sanctuaries at sunrise and sunset , particularly the former, considerably enhances the experience, but would add to the time spent. Where appropriate, the recommended itineraries take into account these times of the day. While rising before dawn to drive for half-an-hour or an hour to a site may not appeal to everyone, the rewards are considerable, being able to watch the first rays of the sun strike the tower or gopura at a pleasantly cool time of the day (midday temperatures, particularly in the summer, can be fierce). Also, visitors wanting to study sanctuaries in detail, particularly Phimai and Phnom Rung, should allow more than the recommended times.

One-night itinerary

Leave Bangkok in the morning, stopping for lunch at one of the lakeside restaurants overlooking the Lam Takhong reservoir if travelling by car. Alterntively, the morning express train from Bangkok arrives in Khorat in the early afternoon, or there is a 45-minute flight from Don Muang airport. Stop briefly in Khorat to check in at the hotel, and then drive up to Phimai via Route 2, turning right after 49 km at Thalad Kae; the town of Phimai lies 12 km further on, with the temple close to its centre. Spend the rest of the afternoon at the sanctuary (it closes before dusk), optionally visiting the Phimai Museum, a short drive back along the same road but still within the town. Like most museums in the country, it is closed on Mondays, Tuesdays and public holidays.

For sunset, return along the same road in the direction of Khorat to Phnom Wan. Exactly at the 15 km marker, a sign on the left indicates a small road leading to Phnom Wan, 5 km beyond. Return to Khorat for the night.

Early the next morning, drive directly to Phnom Rung, 126 km to the east. Take Routes 224 and 24 to the village of Ban Tako, 14 km beyond Nang Rong, and turn right onto Route 2117. After 5 km turn right onto Route 2221, which leads directly up the hill. If the weather is clear, make every effort to arrive as early as possible - the approach on foot, up the succession of staircases, leads to the complex main eastern gopura, which looks incomparable as it catches the first rays of the sun rising over the flat plains to the east. Have breakfast at one of the several foodstalls on the road leading down from the sanctuary, and drive on to Muang Tam, a 10-minute drive to the south along signposted country roads. Just before entering the small village that surrounds the sanctuary, the road skirts a large rectangular lake, the Khmer baray that has been in continuous use since it was built as an adjunct to Muang Tam.

Return along the same route, to Khorat and back along Route 2 to Bangkok. 32 km from Khorat, turn right onto Route 2161, signposed to Amphoe Sung Noen. After 2 $^1/_2$ km, just before Sung noen village, turn right; continue on this road, which curves left after 2 km and crosses the main Northeast railway line (unguarded crossing). From the railway line, Non Ku lies 800 m ahead, immediately to the right of the road, Muang Khaek lies 500 m. These two sanctuaries merit only a brief visit, but but the short detour is worthwhile. Also en route, back on Route 2 and 1 km further on, is the stone quarry of Si Khiu. A car park on the left marks the site; a short flight of steps above this leads to the deeply-incised pattern of massive grey sandstone, giving every impression that the masons have only just stopped work.

Three-night itinerary including Preah Vihear

Assumming that conditions allow a visit to Preah Vihear, begin east as for the one-night intinerary, staying in Khorat and visiting Phimai, Phnom Wan, Phnom Rung and Muang Tam, as above. Return to Prakhon Chai, turn right along Route 24 and drive to its junction with Route 214 at Prasat. Here, turn left and drive 30 km to Surin, to check in at the hotel and have lunch. Mid-afternoon, but no later than about 3.00 pm, drive south back down Route 24. Cross over the junction with Route 24 and 3 km further on turn down a lane opposite the 32 km marker signposted to Ban Phluang, nearly a kilometre at the end, after a final sharp right turn.

Back on Route 24, continue south, turning right after 15 km onto Route 2121. After 35 km, at the village of Ta Mieng, turn left, continuing south for a short distance to an army post. It may be necessary here to ask for permission to continue. The sites of Ta Muen, Ta Muen Toch and, a little beyond, Ta Muen Thom lie in mature forest almost on the escarpment of the Dongrek Range. While the sites themselves are perfectly safe, anti-personnel mines from the 1980s make any overgrown areas along the border a hazard. The steps down from Ta Muen Thom lead into Cambodia. Stay until just before sunset. Return to Surin for the night.

The next morning leave Surin as early as possible on Route 226, heading east towards Sisaket. A 30-minute drive reaches the village of Sikhoraphum. Set back on the left of the road, on the eastern edge of the village in an open, moated area, stands the group of five brick towers on low platform. The rural setting adds to the charm of the site, particularly attractive at or close to sunrise. Continue east for about another 30 minutes until the village of Ban Kamphaeng Yai where the road crosses the railway line. The sanctuary of Kamphaeng Yai is hidden from the road; turn right into the village and head for the modern wat with its prominent, steeply gabled viharn and garish cement iconography. The Khmer sanctuary is within the grounds, surrounded by the massive dark sandstone walls which gave it the name it is now known by (literally, 'Large Walls').

From Kamphaeng Yai, continue east along Route 226. After 18 km, on the left, the road passes by the small laterite prasat of Kamphaeng Noi, worth a brief stop. At Sisaket, turn south along Route 221 and continue all the way to the end, 98 km away where the road finally climbs to a car park and check-point. Leave the car here, fill in the necessary papers on the Thai side (you will need your passort) and continue on foot. A path leads across the bare sandstone to a small bridge over a stream. The first flight of steps that marks the ascent of the sanctuary begins just beyond here. Allow at last two hours for the visit. Return to Kantharalak, enter the town and take the small Route 2085 leading north, and follow the signs to Ubon. Stay the night there.

On the fourth morning, drive south on Route 24; the road turns sharply west at Det Udom. Continue for 181 km from Ubon, until the junction with Route 2124 and turn left. 8 km south of the main kighway is the quiet village of Ban Dom, and in its centre, in open space surrounded by tall palms, is Prasat Phumphon, the country's oldest surviving Khmer sanctuary in good condition. Return to Bangkok by retracing the road to Sangkha, taking Route 24 to Khorat and then Route 2. Stop at Non Ku, Muang Khaek and the Si Khiu quarry, as described at the end of the one-night itinerary.

Two-night itinerary without Preah Vihear

Follow the three-night itinerary as far as Kamphaeng Yai, but then return as far as Sikhoraphum, and turn left at the crossroads onto Route 2371 and drive to the small town of Sangkha, another 38 km distant. Continue directly south, crossing the main highway, Route 24, to Prasat Phumphon, and resume the three-night itinerary.

Adding the border temples around Aranyaprathet

The two sites near Aranyaprathet, Prasat Khao Noi and Sdok Kok Thom, can be reached directly from Bangkok on a long day trip, or by adding to one of the above itineraries as a longish detour. This latter alternative involves driving south from Muang Tam through Ban Kruat (with the option of visiting the kiln sites and quarries) and Laharnsai to Aranyaprathet. The return from there to Bangkok along Route 33 makes it an easy matter to stop at Prachinburi to visit the museum (the Khao Noi lintels are especially worth seeing). The disadvantage of this detour is that it cuts out the visit to Non Ku, Muang Khaek and the Si Khiu quarry on the return to Bangkok. These, however, could be visited on the way up to Khorat at the start of a trip, though this would make a long first day.

The West

Although Muang Singh can be visited as a day trip (the road journey is only about one-and-a-half hours), the trip can also be combined with seeing the River Kwai. The train to Kanchanaburi passes Tha Kilen station, close to Prasat Muang Singh. There are two non-express trains a day, taking 3 1/2 hours; a morning departure from Bangkok and afternoon return from Tha Kilen allows just over two hours at the site, which is ample time. Air-conditioned buses leave Bangkok for Kanchanaburi every 15 minutes.

Museums

The major Thai collections of Khmer pieces are at the National Museum in Bangkok, the Mahavirawong Museum in Khorat, Phimai National Museum, Ubon Ratchathani National Museum and Khonkaen National Museum. All are open Wednesdays to Sundays, except for public holidays.

PLANS OF THE TEMPLES

The plans of the temples presented on the following pages are arranged in the same running order in which the temples appear in the text. They are intended as a rough indication of the layout of each temple and are orientated with North being the top of the page. In general the areas in solid black represent the portions of each temple still existent today while the lighter lines are intended to show the reader how the temple was originally designed.

They have been compiled from a variety of different sources, which accounts for their divergence in style and scale. In addition, given the great difference in actual size of such temples as Preah Vihear and Prasat Ta Muen Thom on page 331, for example, it would have been impossible to fit the two on to the same page had they been drawn to scale.

PRASAT KHAO NOI

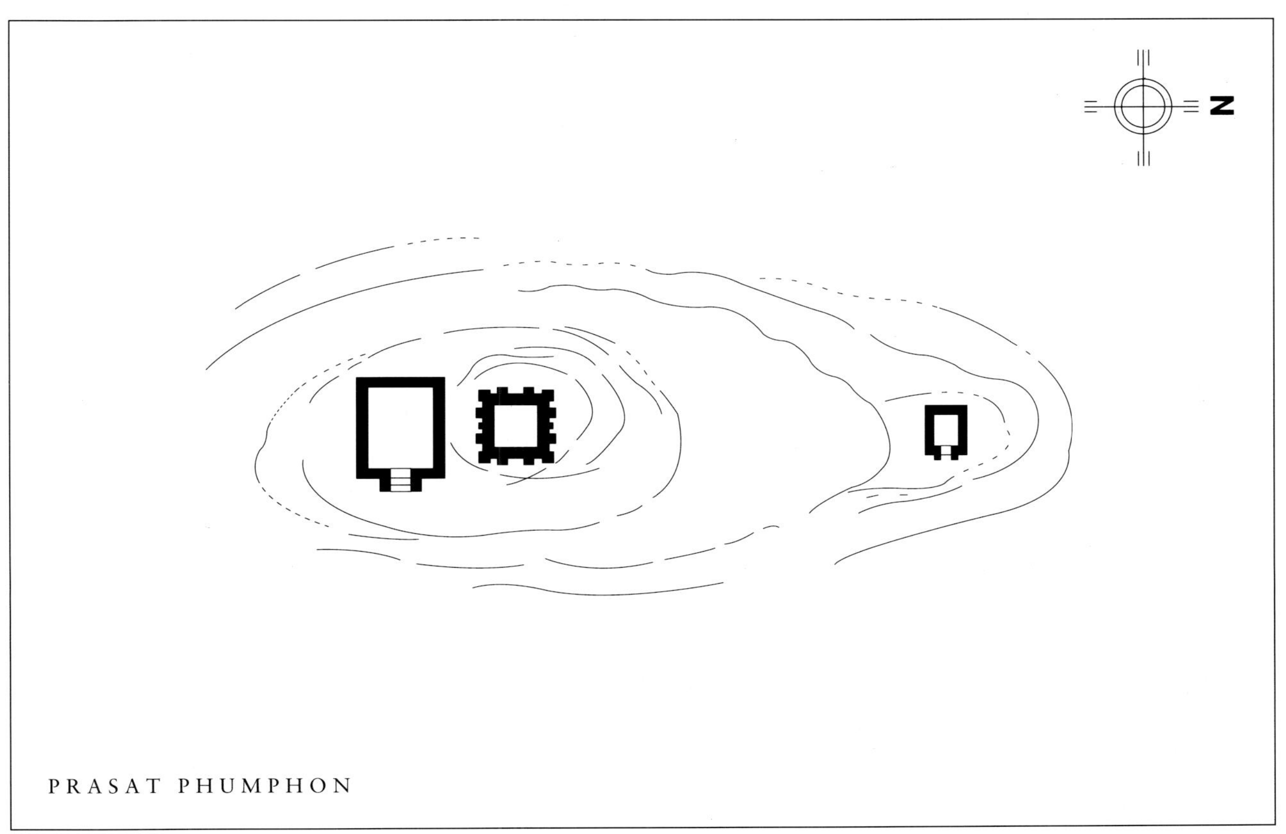

PRASAT PHUMPHON

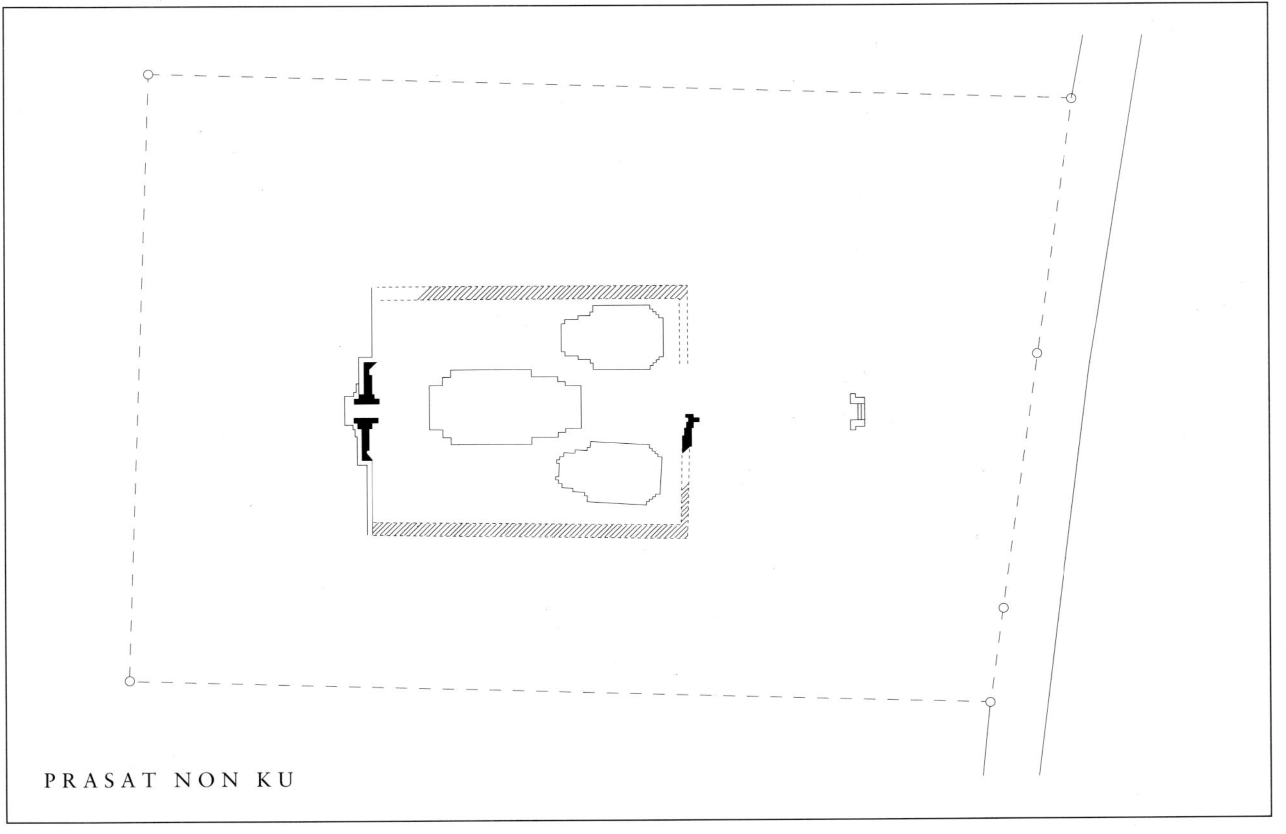

PRASAT NON KU

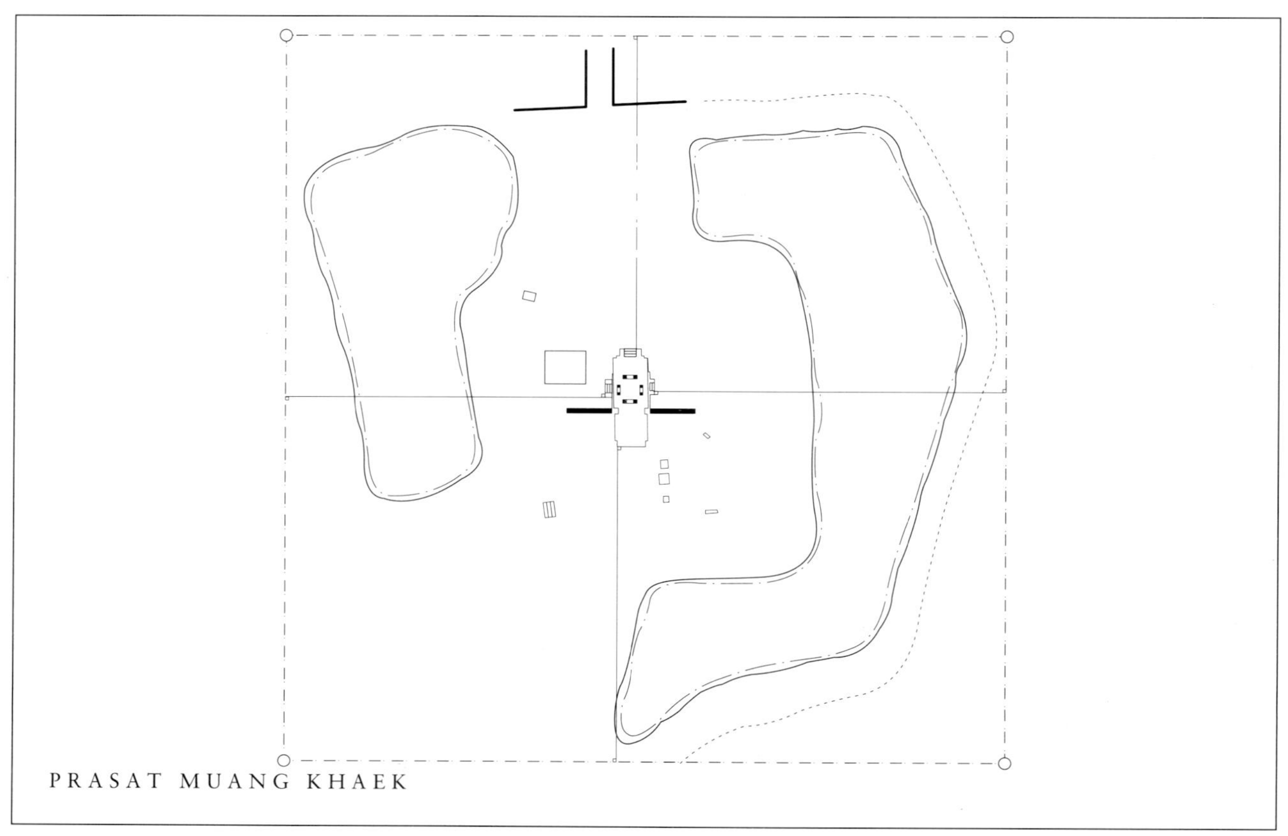
PRASAT MUANG KHAEK

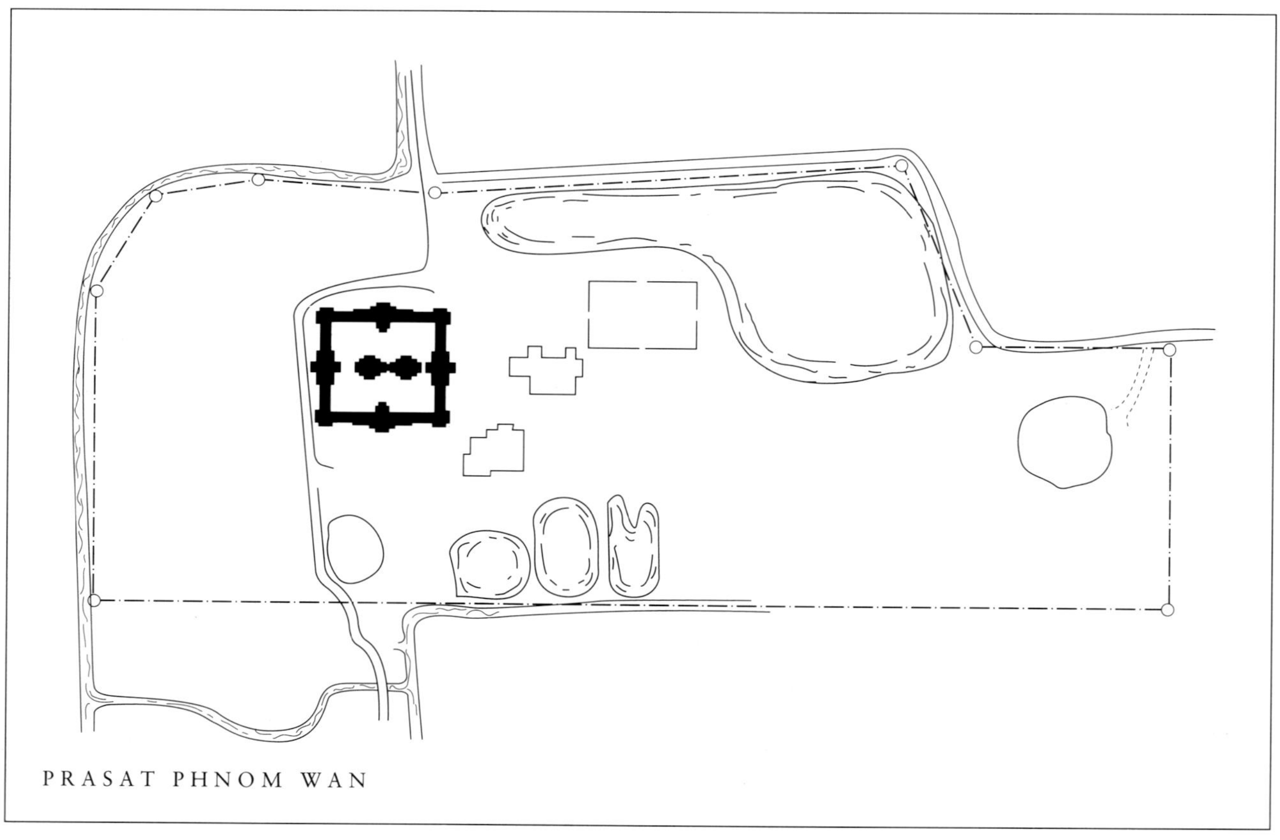
PRASAT PHNOM WAN

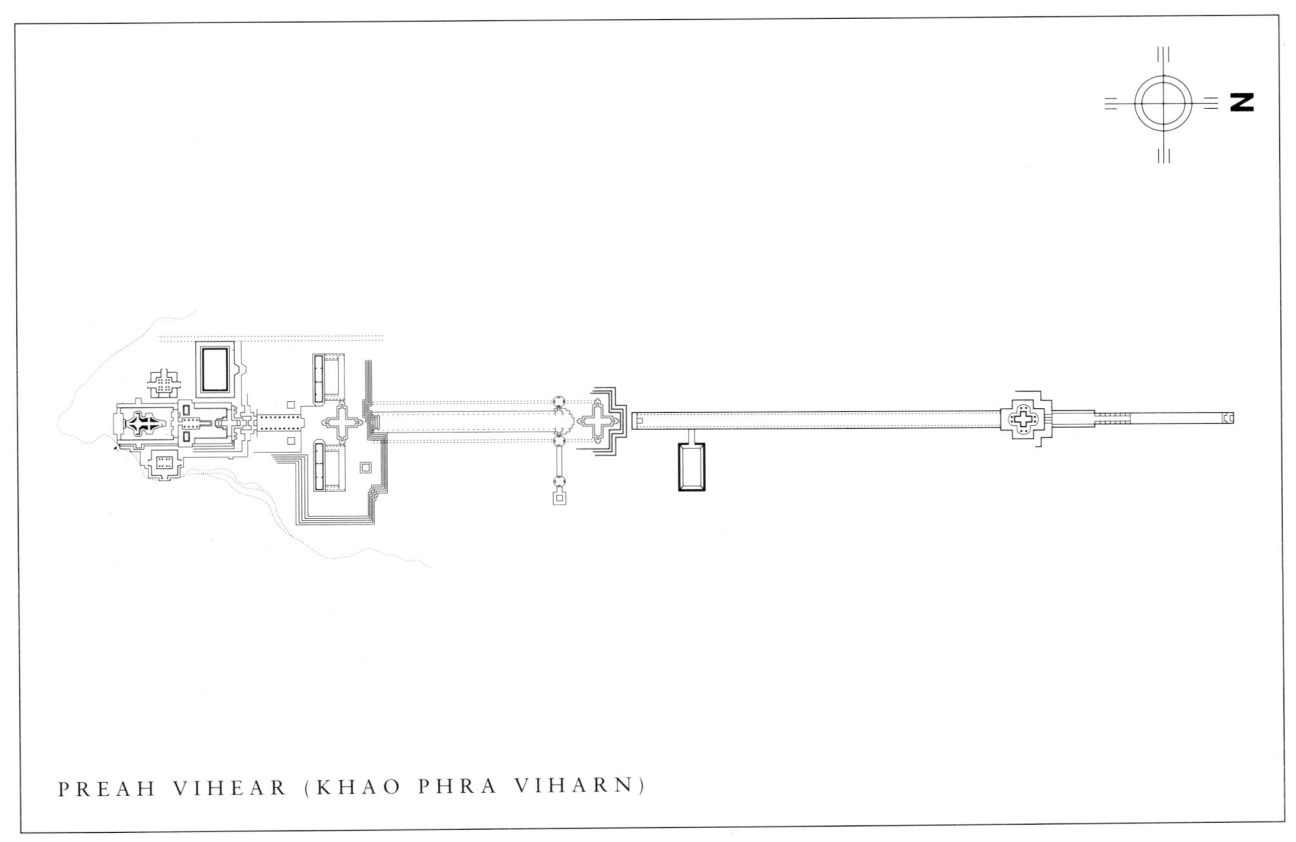

PREAH VIHEAR (KHAO PHRA VIHARN)

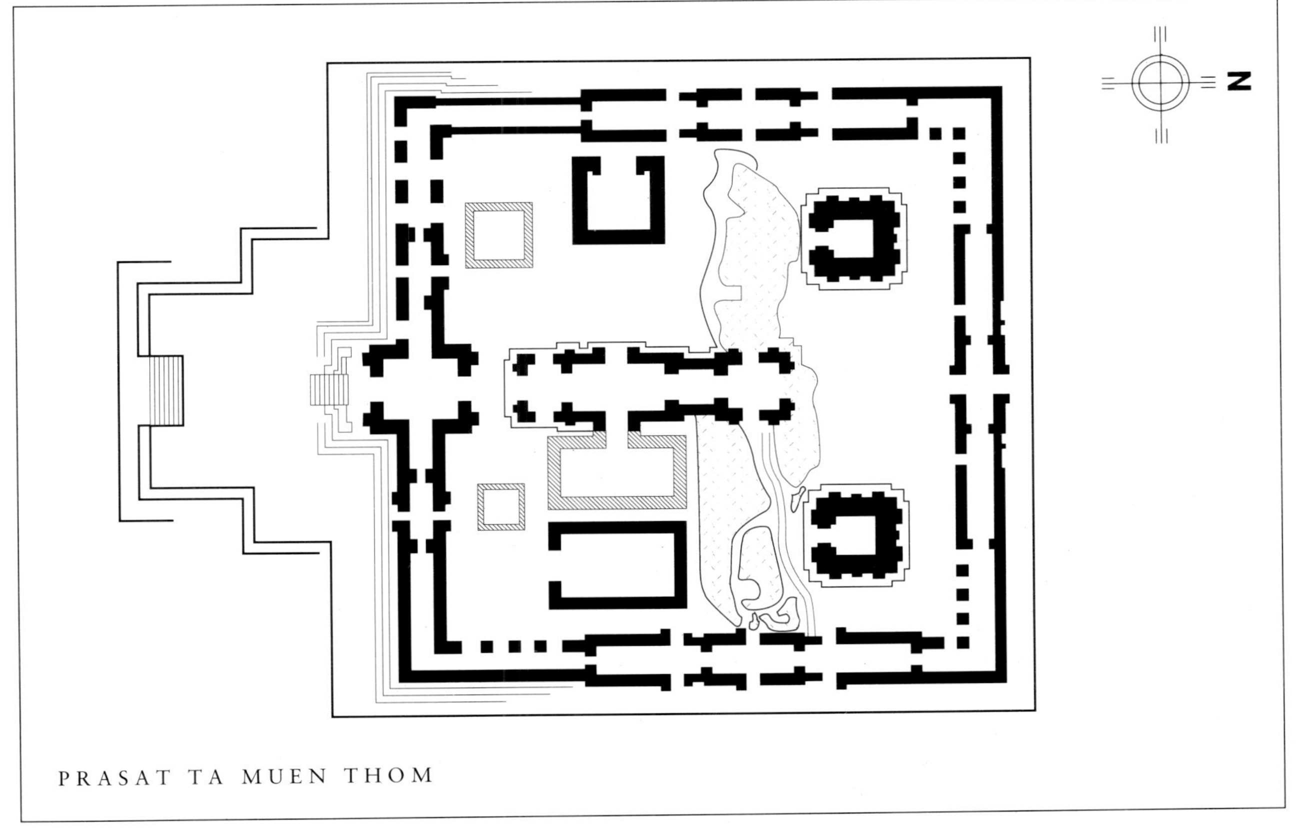

PRASAT TA MUEN THOM

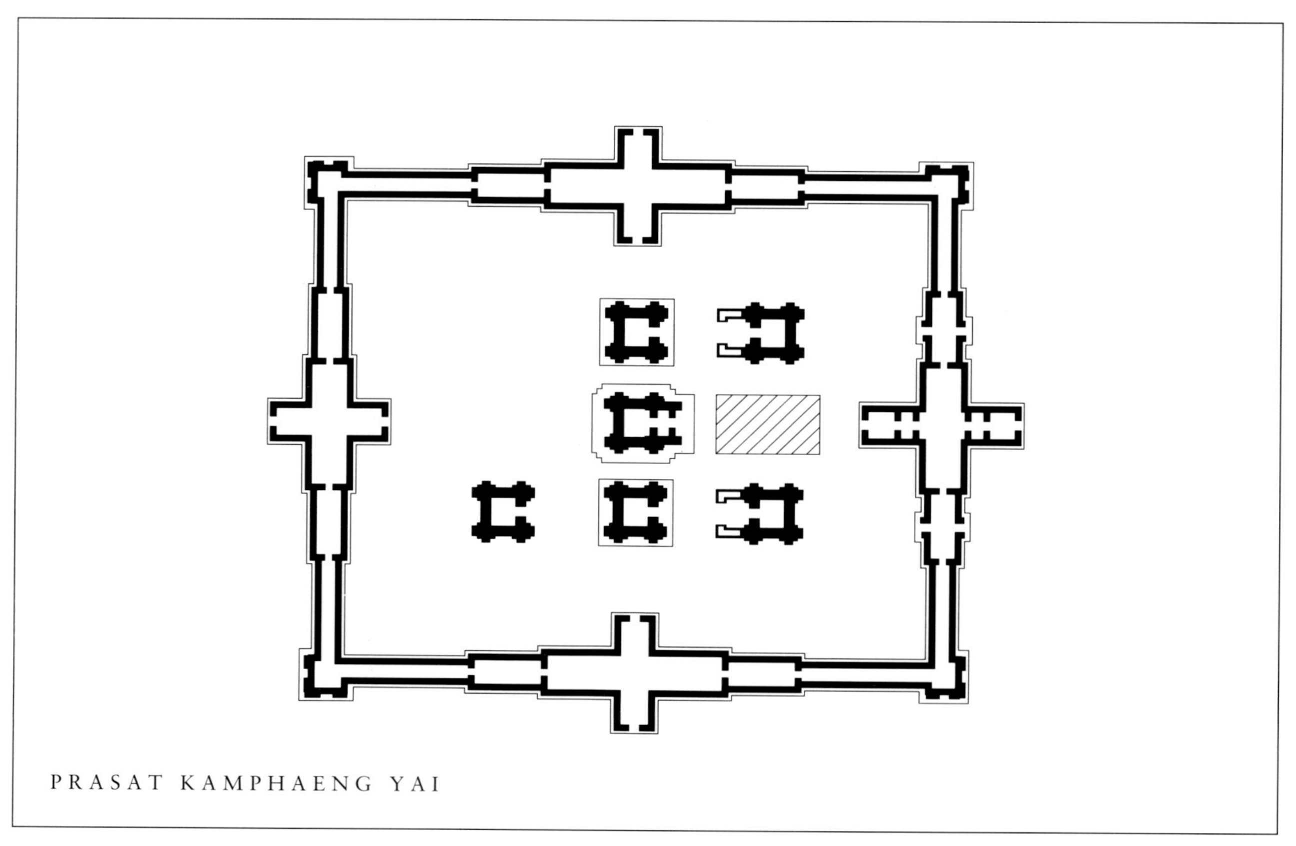

PRASAT KAMPHAENG YAI

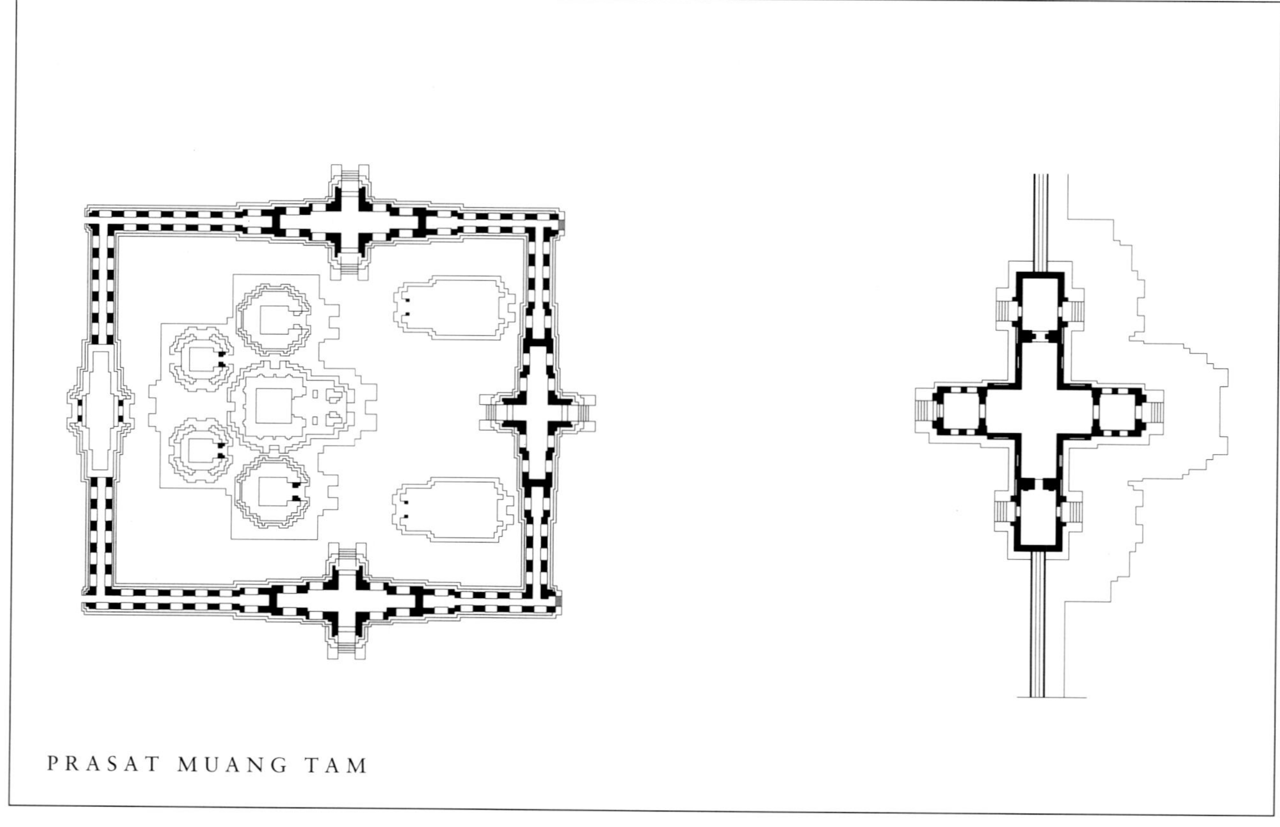

PRASAT MUANG TAM

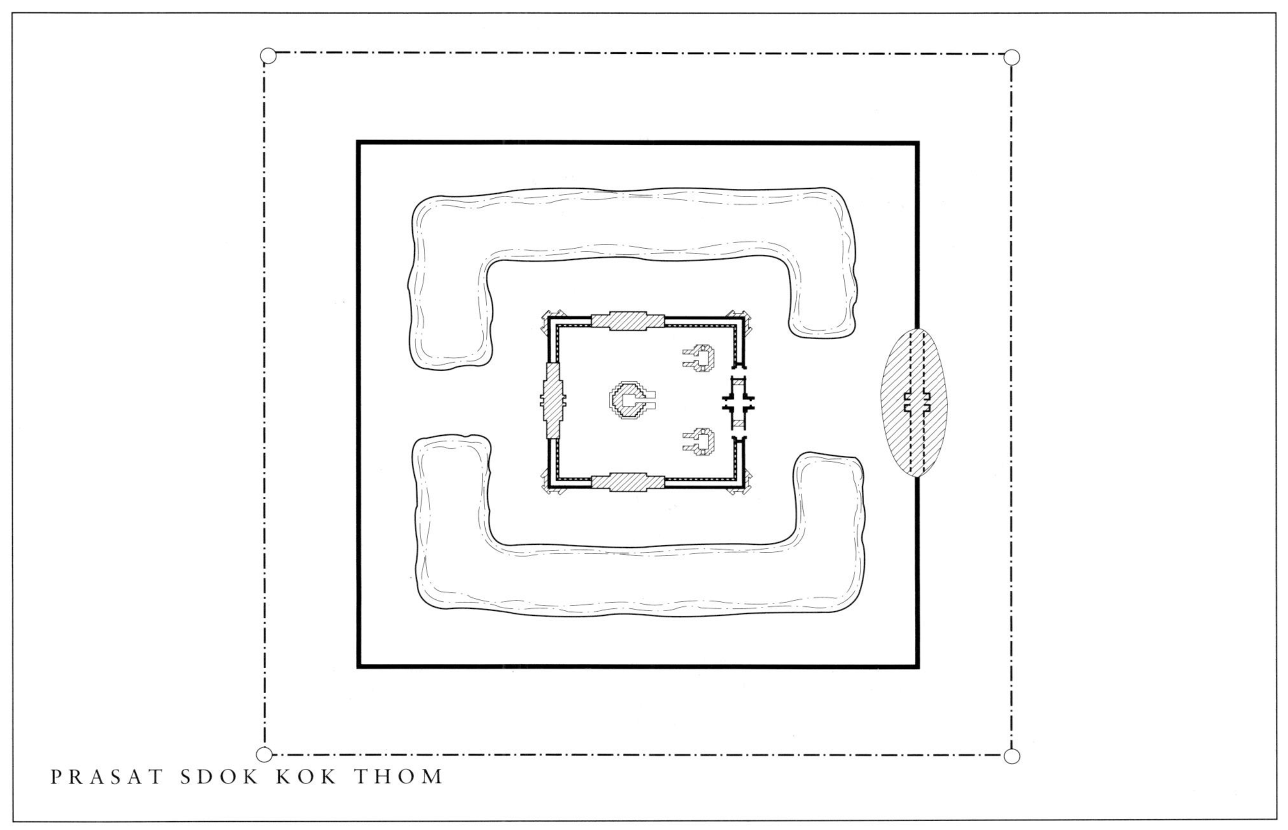

PRASAT SDOK KOK THOM

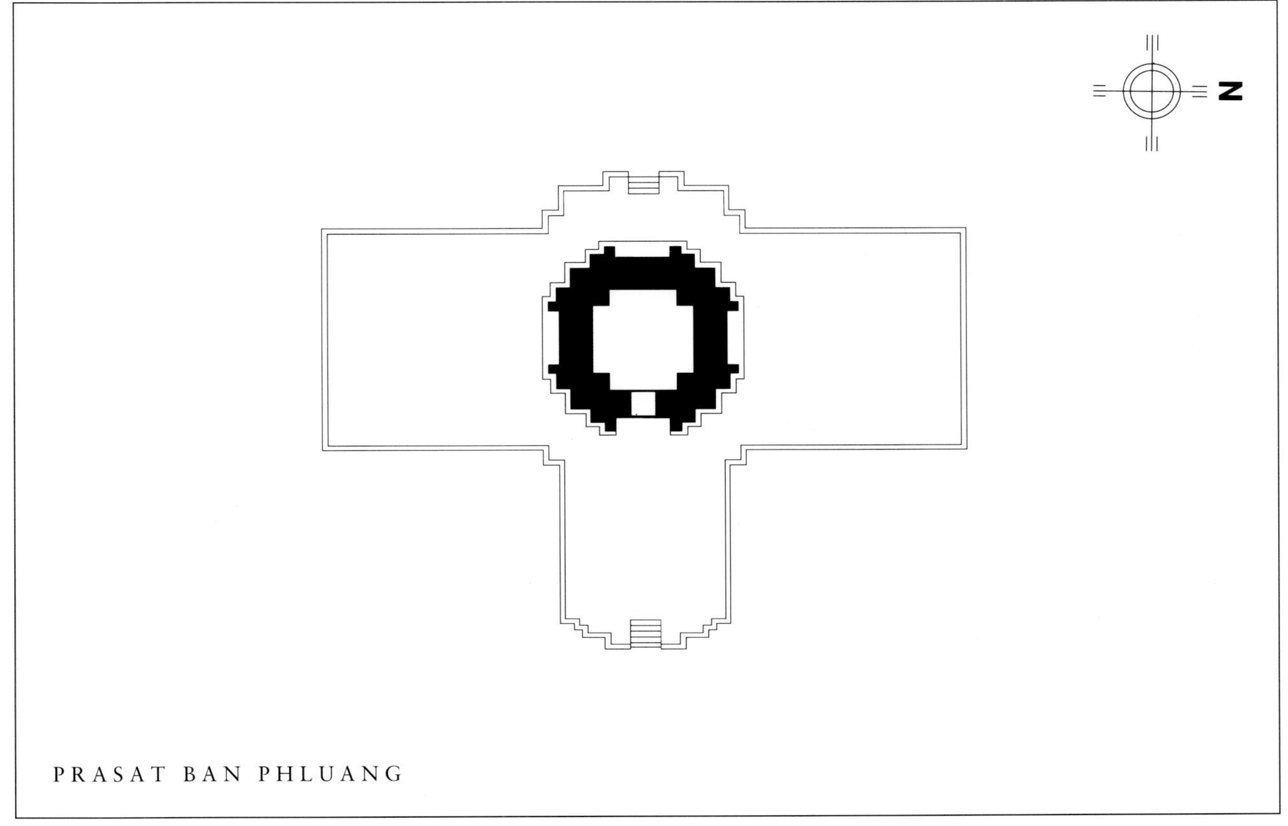

PRASAT BAN PHLUANG

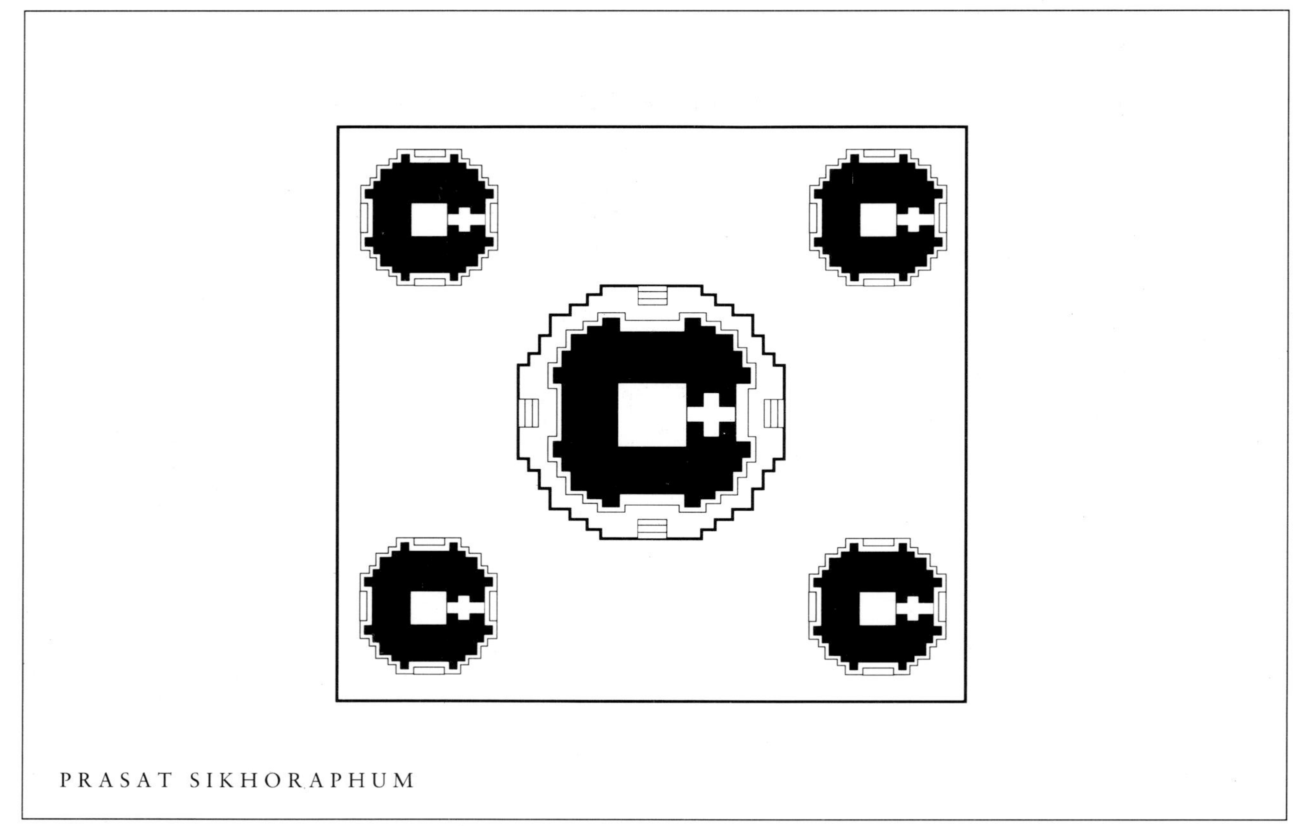

PRASAT SIKHORAPHUM

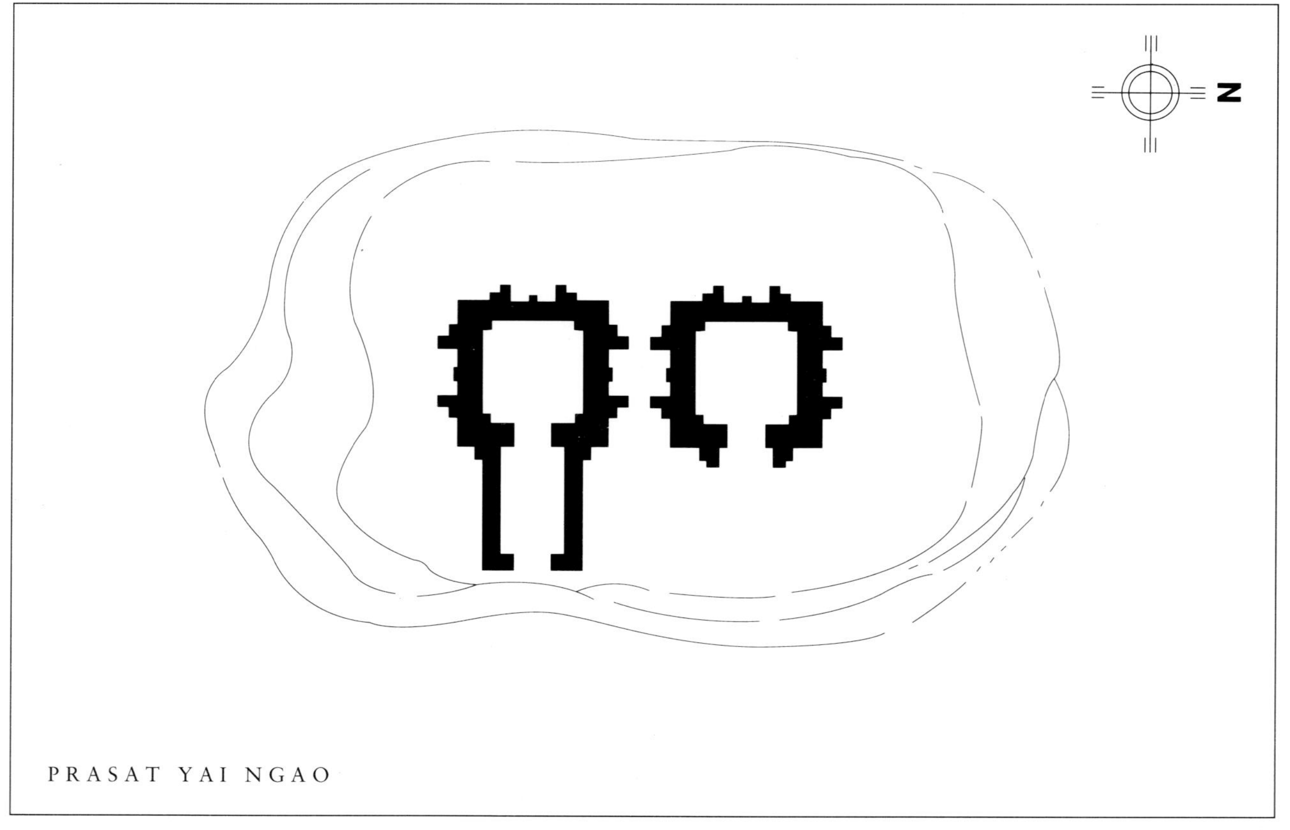

PRASAT YAI NGAO

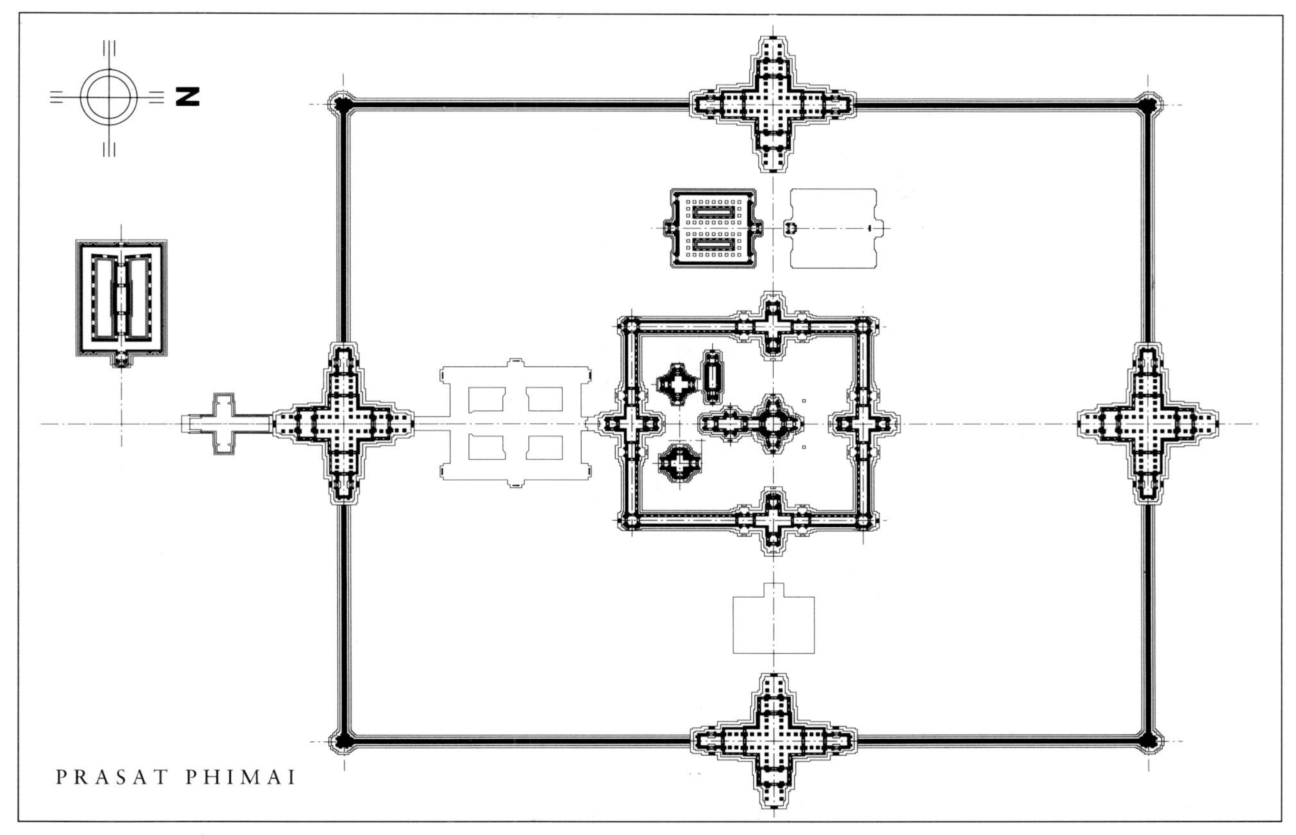

PRASAT PHIMAI

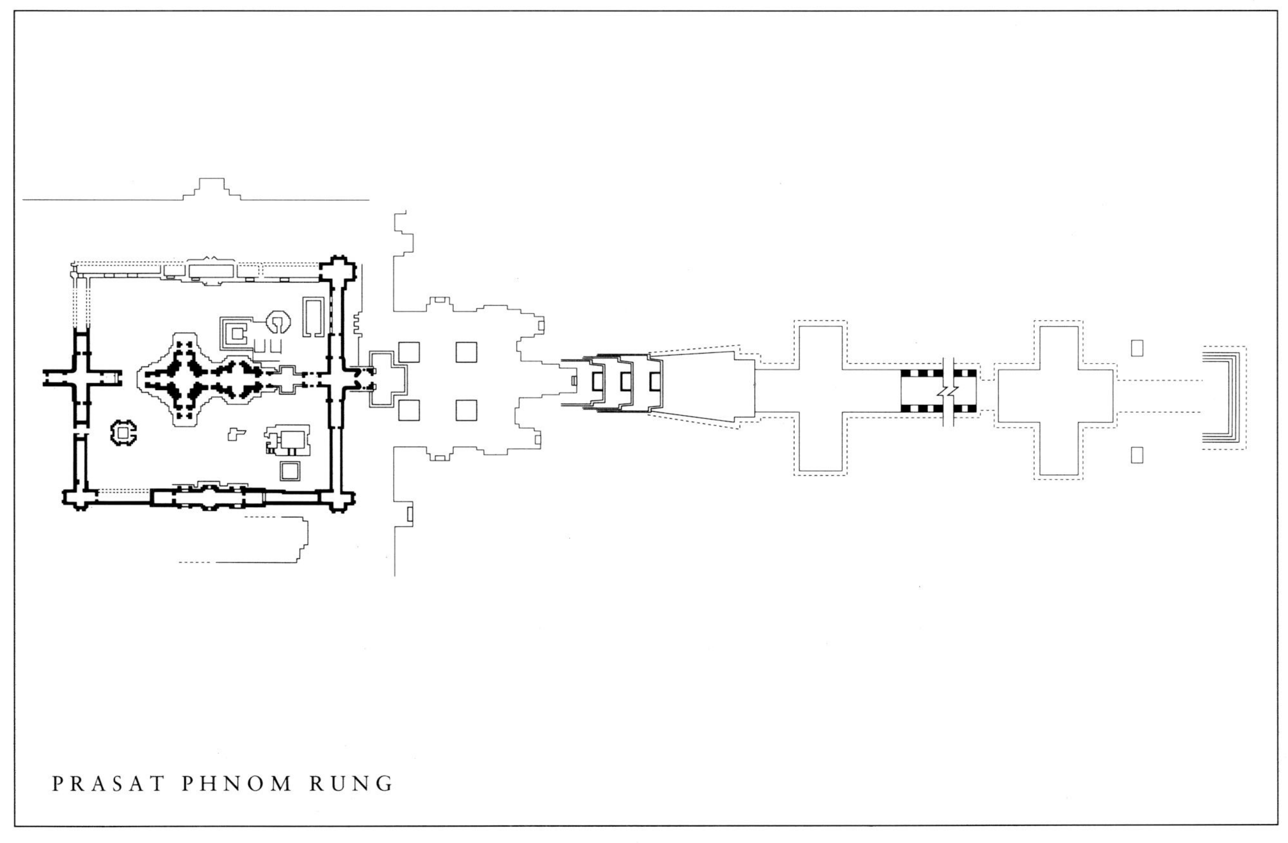

PRASAT PHNOM RUNG

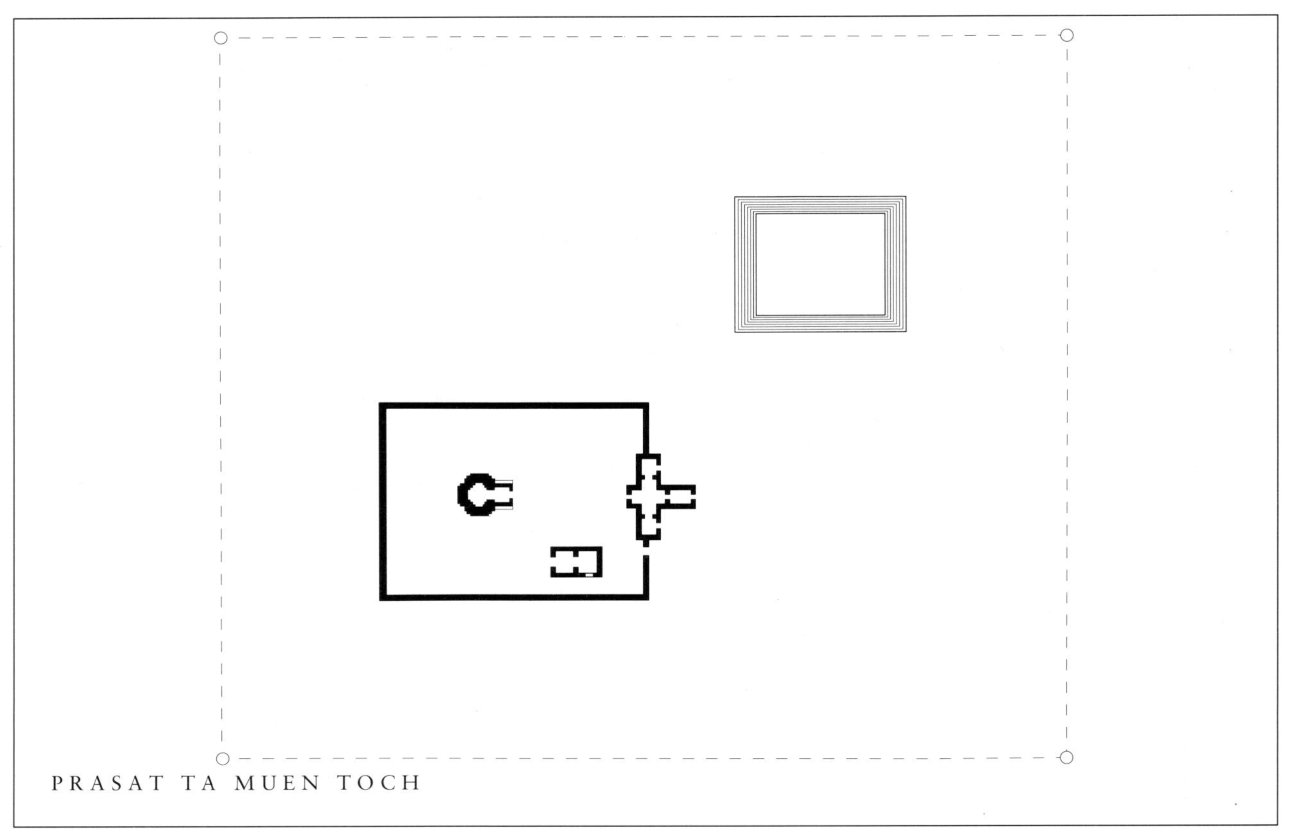

PRASAT TA MUEN TOCH

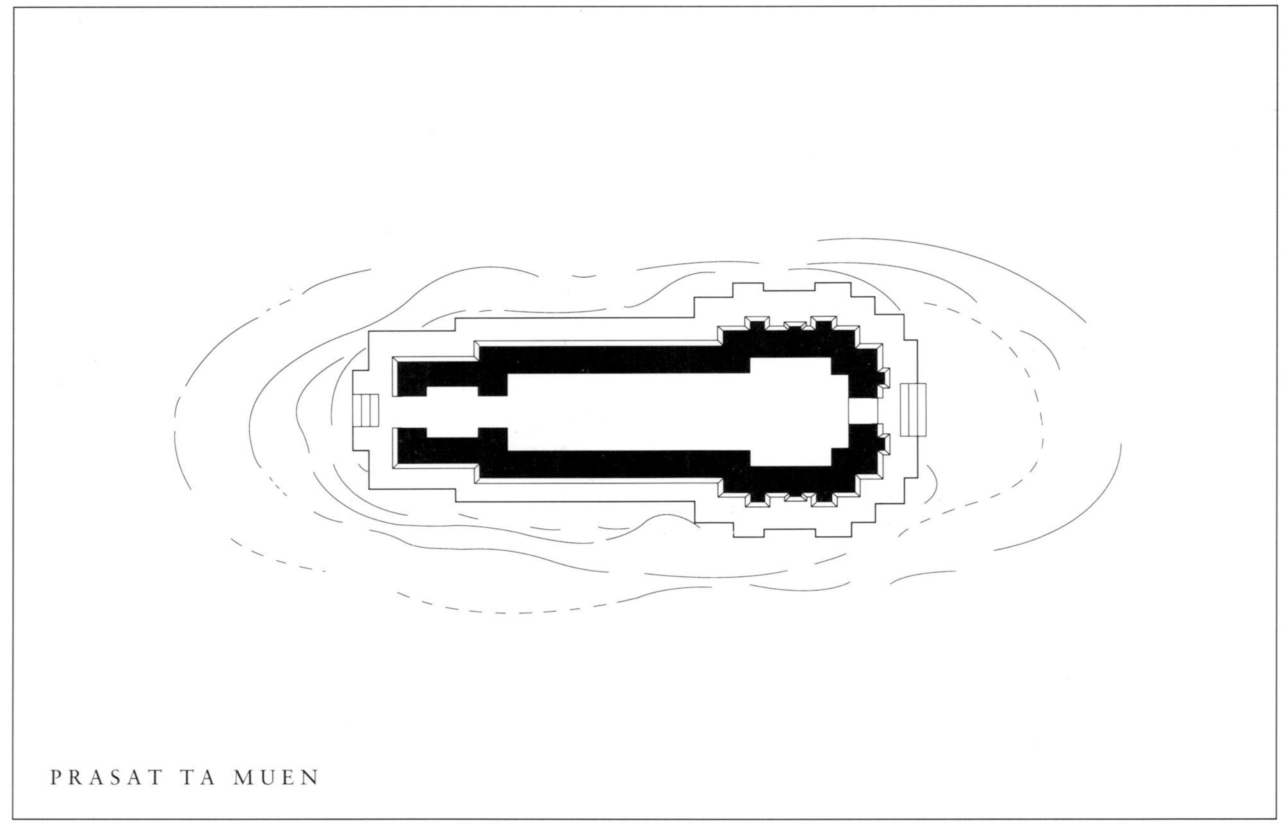

PRASAT TA MUEN

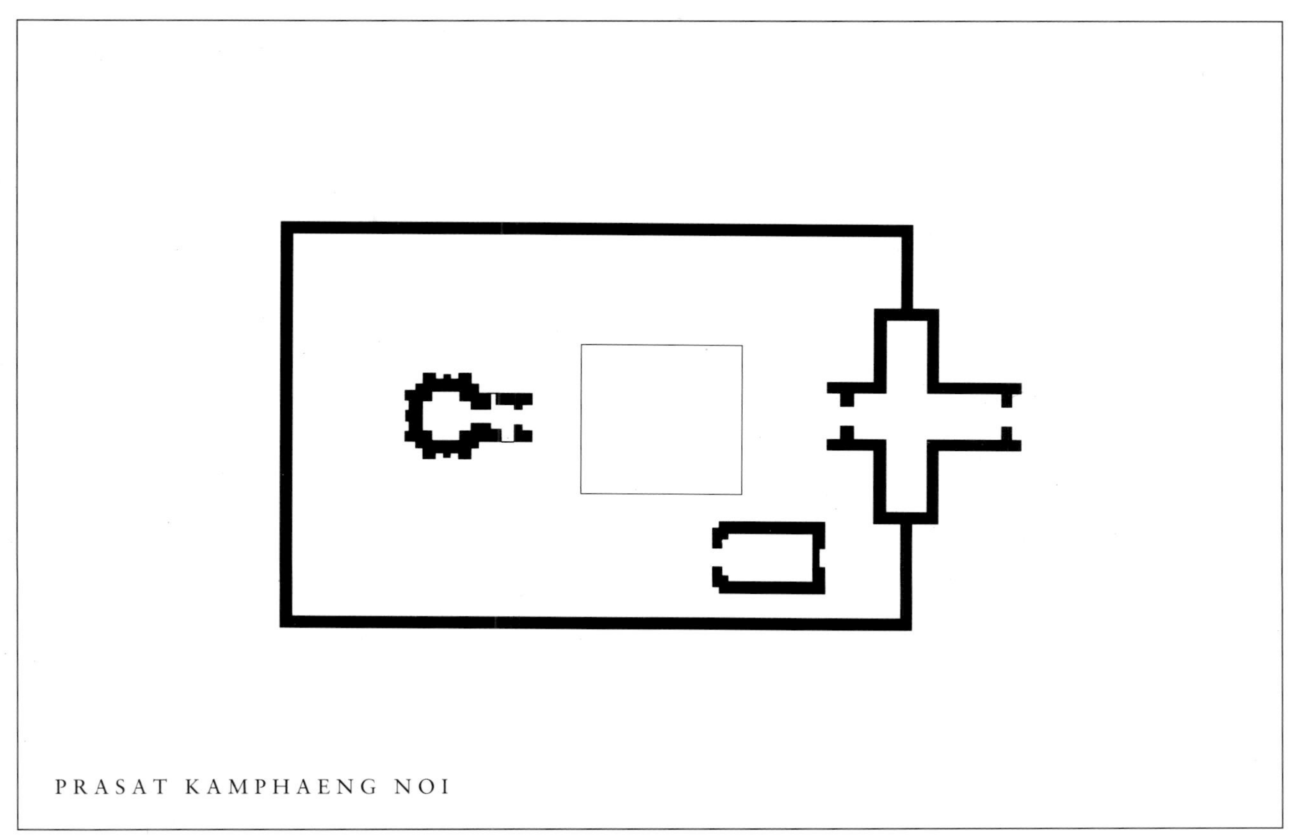

PRASAT KAMPHAENG NOI

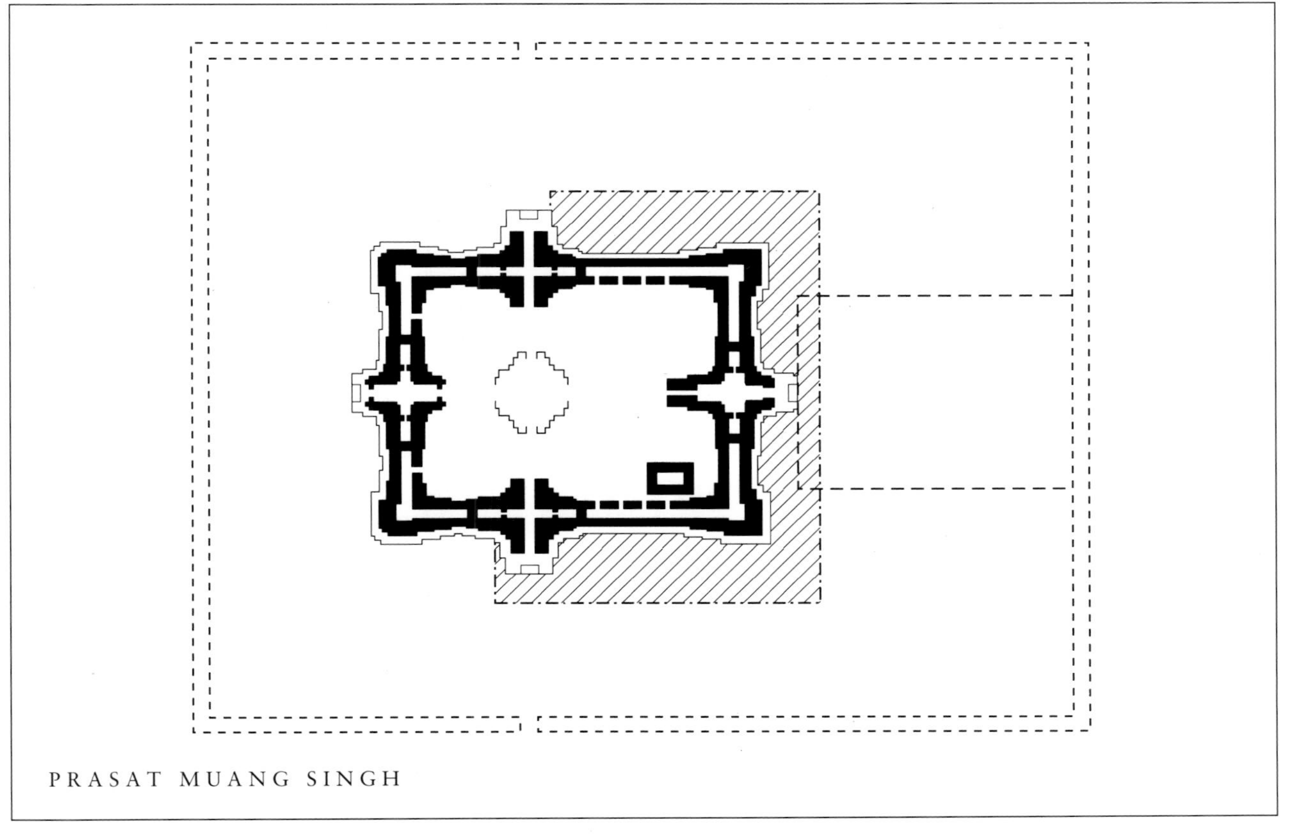

PRASAT MUANG SINGH

NOTES ON THE PHOTOGRAPHY

Above
Michael Freeman

Opposite
The view looking east along the escarpment of the Dongret Mountains from Gopura III on Preah Vihear.

The principal photography of the temples took place in just over twelve months from March 1990 and, for the most part, our sorties were controlled by the light. For such enduring places, their appearance and atmosphere undergo remarkable changes through the seasons and in the course of a day. The early mornings, before and after sunrise and the evenings were nearly always the most evocative times. Partly this was because of the speed with which the sun in the tropics rises and sets: for most of the day it is so high that, in clear weather, it produces the strange combination of deep local shadows and a visual flatness from a distance.

Partly also, the early morning was a favoured time because of the way in which the temples were built, most facing east. Usually the best facades and the best views catch the sun as it rises. There was also the matter of weather and season. The detail in the stonework, always important, seemed to demand a raking, direct light to bring it out, and this can only be relied upon in the dry season.

To an extent, we also had to schedule our visits according to restoration work in its various stages, Phimai and Phnom Rung, the two major sites, had already been completed after lengthy work. It would have been impossible to start during their restoration. Then, however, as part of new central government investment in the Northeast, restoration projects sprang up for a number of smaller Khmer monuments that had so far languished for centuries. Whether one prefers restored or untouched temples, during the work itself they tend to look like building sites. In certain cases we had little time to lose; in others, the camera position needed to be chosen with care.

Temples of such presence as these called for large-format photography and nearly all of the the large views were shot on either 4 x 5 inch film, or 6 x 9 cm rollfilm, mainly with a wide-angle 65 mm lens on a Sinar camera. Details and photographs that needed a telephoto lens, were shot on fine-grained 35 mm film.

Not all the photographic trips were straightforward. Indeed, that to Preah Vihear (Khao Phra Viharn) seemed highly unlikely at the start, progressed to merely unlikely in the last month, and only came in sight on the day we were able to reach it. Political circumstances were still difficult. On another occasion and another temple we were escorted by a unit of soldiers with a mine detector and an Alsation (also, as it turned out, a mine detector).

All those responsible for maintaining the sites, the museum staff in Bangkok, Nakhon Ratchasima, Phimai, Khonkaen, Ubon Ratchathani and Prachinburi and members of the Fine Arts Department did more than we asked of them to make the photography possible. My special thanks also go to Paisarn Piemmettawat, Patra Khan and Mana Aramsri, who accompanied me on these trips.

GLOSSARY

Abhaya mudra The mudra, or gesture, of reassurance, in which the palm of the right hand is held outward with the fingers extended upward.

Adi-Buddha The predominant Buddha in Mahayana Buddhism.

Airavata The elephant, mount or vehicle of Indra, usually portrayed with three heads, but occasionally with one only. Known in Thai as Erawan.

Agni The Vedic god of fire and one of the three principal gods in the Rig Veda (with Indra and Surya). Agni grants immortality and cleanses sin, and mediates between the gods and men.

Amitabha The Bhodisattva of infinite light, who helps those who falter and are weak.

Amrita The elixir of life, or ambrosia, produced by the Churning of the Sea of Milk, and over which the gods and demons fought. Literally, 'non-dead'. May also be the same as 'soma'.

Ananta The endless World Serpent floating in the cosmic sea, and supporting Vishnu as he sleeps through the night of Brahma before the rebirth of the world. Also known as Sesha.

Anantasayin Term used for reclining Vishnu on the back of the Naga Ananta.

Antaravasaka Lower garment (of three) for Buddhist monks.

Aspsaras Celestial dancers who entertain the gods and are the sensual rewards of kings and heroes who die bravely. In Hindu mythology they always performed with the celestial musicians, gandharvas, but in Khmer mythology they were elevated alone to special importance in temple decoration.

Arishta Demon in the form of an ox, sent to kill Krishna by his uncle Kamsa.

Asura Demon, and enemy of the gods. Asuras and gods are locked in perpetual conflict, although in the Churning of the Sea of Milk they act, albeit temporarily, in concert. Asura originally meant something quite different in the Rig Veda - a divine being.

Avalokitesvara The Compassionate Bodhisattva, also known as Lokesvara. He is the Mahayana Buddhist ideal of compassion, choosing not to pass into nirvana but to help instead to bring enlightenment to humans.
Often represented as a young man holding a lotus in his left hand and wearing an image of the Bodhisattva Amitabha on his head.

Avatar The 'descent' or incarnation of a god, in the form of a human or animal. Rama, for instance, is one of the avatars of Vishnu.

Balarama Half-brother of Rama - the serpent Ananta in human form.

Bali The brother of the monkey-king Surgriva who usurped the latter's throne in the Ramayana epic.

Banaspati Mythical animal in Dvaravati art with horns, wings and beak.

Bhadresvara Alternative name for Shiva

Bhaisajyaguru Name given to a Mahayan Buddha considered the master of medicine, worshipped in the arogayasala.

Bhumidevi Goddess of the Earth and one of the two consorts of Vishnu.

Bhumisparsa mudra The mudra, or gesture, of touching the Earth. With this mudra, Buddha called the Earth-goddess to witness. From 'bhumi' meaning Earth.

Bodhisattva In Mahayana Buddhism, a being who voluntarily stops short of reaching Buddhahood in order to help humanity. The stage in the development of a Buddha before Enlightenment.

Brahma The Creator of all things, originally conceived as the deification of Brahma, becoming the principal deity of the Trimurti (with Vishnu and Shiva). Brahma has four heads and four arms, holding sceptre, rosary, bow and alms-bowl. Brahma is born from Vishnu's navel at the beginning of each world cycle. His vehicle is the hamsa, or goose.

Brahman The transcendent absolute.

Brahmani See Brahmi.

Brahmi One of the Sapta Matrikas (Seven Divine Mothers); also called Brahmani.

Brahmin Hindu priest.

Bringin Legendary disciple of Shiva.

Buddha 'The Enlightened One'. Gautama Siddartha, born in 543 BC.

Cakra The wheel, emblem of Buddhist law and of the sun.

Cakravala The concentric rings of mountain ranges which enclose the world mountain Meru, in Hindu cosmology.

Cakravartin Universal ruler.

Chenla The Chinese name for Cambodia.

Chola A style of Indian art from the period 900-1287 AD.

Deva Deity.

Devaki Krishna's mother.

Devaraja Meaning god who is king, a cult deriving from Shiva-worship in which the king had divine associations.

Devata Lesser deity.

Devi Goddess and consort of Shiva in her benevolent form. Also known as Uma, Gauri, Parvati, Jaganmata.See also Durhga.

Dhana-mudra The attitude of meditation, in which both hands, fingers extended, rest in the lap right above left.

Dhanwantali Celestial doctor, a minor form of Vishnu.

Dharani The earth goddess.

Dharma The doctrine of Hindu moral duty. Also, an ancient rishi.

Dharmacakra The Buddhist Wheel of the Law, representing the dominion of the Buddha's Law over everything.

Dharmacakra-mudra The gesture of teaching, or turning the Dharmacakra, in which both hands are held iogether in front of the chest, the thumb and index finger joined. The right hand represents the wheel of the Law, the left hand is in the action of turning it.

Dharni An orb representing the earth, frequently held by Uma.

Dikpalaka The gods of direction who guarded the four directions - north, south, east and west.

Durga Consort of Shiva in her terrible form. Also called Kali.

Dvarapala Temple guardian, normally scupted as a door watchman.

Dvaravati Name given to the culture and art widespread throughout Thailand from the 6th to 11th centuries.

Erawan Thai name for Airavata.

Funan The oldest Indianised state of Indochina and precursor of Chenla.

Gaja Elephant.

Gajasimha Part elephant, part lion.

Gana Servant of Shiva, the leader of which group is Ganesha.

Gandharva Celestial musician, normally associated with apsaras.

Ganesha Elephant-headed son of Shiva. According to legend, Shiva decapitated his son in a moment of anger and in remorse replaced the head with the first that came to hand - that of an elephant.

Garuda Mythical bird-man; the vehicle of Vishnu. Mortal enemy of the nagas.

Gopala An alternative name for Krishna; also, the name for a cow-herd (Krishna lived as one as a youth to escape his uncle).

Govardhana The mountain that Krishna lifts to protect the cow-herds and their cattle from Indra's rain.

Guru Brahmin spiritual instructor.

Hamsa Sacred goose; vehicle of Brahma. In Buddhism represents the flight of the doctrine. Also means 'soul'.

Hanuman Monkey general and ally of Rama in the Ramayana.

Hara Alternative name for Shiva.

Hari Alternative name for Vishnu.

Harihara A form of Shiva in which Shiva and Vishnu are combined in one image.

Harivamsa Sacred book containing the genealogy of Hari - that is Vishnu.

Hasatiling Mythical bird living in the Himavatta forest and eating elephants for sustenance.

Himavatta Mythical forest surrounding Mount Meru.

Hinayana 'Lesser Vehicle' referring to the traditional conservative form of Buddhism which concentrates on the doctrine rather than on the worship of the Buddha or Bodhisattvas. Its adherents use the term 'Theravada' instead.

Hiranya A Khmer prince, son of Narendraditya and founder of Phnom Rung.

Hiranyagasipu Demon killed by Vishnu in his avatar Narasimha (man-lion).

Indra The Vedic god of the sky, clouds and monsoon, and guardian of the East. The pricipal god in the Rig Veda.

Isuan Thai pronunciation of Isvara, that is Shiva.

Isvara, -esvara The Lord Shiva, supreme deity.

Indrajita Son of Ravana.

Indrani One of the Sapta Matrikas, or Seven Divine Mothers.

Jataka 'Birth-story' of which there are 547 recounting the Buddha's previous incarnations.

Jatamukuta Hairstyle in the form of a tall chignon, worn by Shiva, Saivite hermits; also worn by Bhodisattvas in Mahayana Buddhism.

Jayabuddhamahanartha Statue of the Buddha made by royal command of Jayavarman VII to be sent to his vassal cities.

Jina Synonym of the Buddha.

Kailasa, Mount Abode of Shiva named after the actual mountain Kailas in western Tibet.

Kala Adopted Indian motif; demon commanded to devour itself. Commonly scupted over a temple entrance as guardian.

Kalasa A pot (a purnakalasa is a pot filled with water and plants, symbolising prosperity - a kind of cornucopia).

Kaliya Name of the naga with multiple heads subdued by Krishna.

Kalkin Future and last avatar of Vishnu.

Kalpa A cycle of time, at the end of which Shiva destroys the world; following this, a new kalpa is initiated by the recreation of the world when Brahma is reborn from the navel of Vishnu. Each kalpa is a day and a night of Brahma, but 8,640 million human years, and contains 2,000 mahayugas, or 'great ages'. See also yuga.

Kamrateng anh Khmer term for a high dignitary (lit. 'my lord').

Kamsa Uncle of Krishna.

Kareikkal-ammeyar Female disciple of Shiva.

Kaumari One of the Sapta Matrikas, or Seven Divine Mothers.

Kesin Demon in the form of a horse sent by Kamsa to kill his nephew Krishna.

Ketumala See Ushnisha.

Kirtimukha Literally 'glory face'. Term used for kala.

Krishna One of the avatars, or incarnations, of Vishnu and hero of the Mahabharata epic.

Krut Cambodian and Thai name for Garuda.

Kshatriya Hindu warrior caste.

Kubera The god who is guardian of the North.

***Kurma** (or kurma-avatara)* One of the avatars, or incarnations, of Vishnu as a giant turtle. Kurma appears supporting Mount Mandara in the Churning of the Sea of Milk.

Kuvalayapida Demon in the form of an elephant sent by Kamsa to kill Krishna.

Lakshmi Wife of Vishnu, goddess of fortune and symbol of Vishnu's creative energy. Her emblem is the lotus.

Lakshmana Brother of Rama.

Lalitasana Seated posture with one leg folded in fornt of the body, the other on the ground - the posture of relaxation.

Lanka Capital city of Ravana.

Linga Stylized image of a phallus representing the essence of the god Shiva. In Sanskirt the word means 'sign' and 'distinguishing symbol'.

Lingaparvata A naturally-occurring mountain, hill or peak in the form of a linga.

Lokesvara See Avalokitesvara.

Mahabharata Major Hindu epic written between about 400 BC and 200 AD with a central narrative of the feud between the Kaurava and Pandava dynasties.

Mahakala One of the guardians of Lord Shiva.

Mahayana 'Great Vehicle' referring to the later form of Buddhism in which the Buddha and Bodhisattvas are worshipped as deities.

Mahesvara An alternative name for Shiva.

Maitreya The future Buddha yet to come.

Makara Sea monster with scales, claws and a large head, often the form of a crocodile, sometimes with the trunk of an elephant. In Khmer sculpture acquired from India via Java.

Mandala Magic diagram in the shape of the cosmos.

Mandara, Mount Mythical mountain used as the pivot for Churning of the Sea of Milk.

Mara The master demon of illusion, the Evil One in Buddhist myth.

Maricha Cousin of Ravana who disguises himself as the Golden Deer to lure Rama away from Sita.

***Matsya**, or matsya-avatara* The incarnation of Vishnu as a fish.

Maya The fundamental illusion of worldly existence.

Meru, Mount The cosmic or world mountain of Hindu cosmology which lies at the centre of the universe. Its summit is the home of the gods. Also called Sumeru.

Mohini Minor form of Vishnu, in which the god disguises himself as a beautiful woman to tempt the demons and so recover the amrita produced by the Churning of the Sea of Milk.

Mon People inhabiting lower Burma, and central Thailand from the 6th to 11th centuries. The Mon culture in Thailand is known as Davaravati.

Muchalinda The giant serpent who shelters the meditating Buddha from a storm with its hood.

Mudra The ritual gesture of the hands of a deity or Buddha.

Mukhalinga Linga with the face of Shiva.

Naga Multi-headed serpent with many mythological connections, associated with water, fertility, rainbows, and creation. Five and seven-headed nagas are common motifs.

Nagapasa A noose in the form of a naga that develops from an arrow fired by Indrajita.

Nagara Indian word for city or capital, the origin of the Khmer word 'Angkor', the Thai derivation of which is 'Nakhon'.

Nagini Serpent goddess.

Nandikesvara See Nandin.

Nandin Sacred bull - the mount, or vehicle, of Shiva.

Narai See Vishnu.

Narasimha, or nrisimha-avatara The avatar, or incarnation, of Vishnu as part-man, part-lion.

Nataraja The cosmic dance performed by Shiva.

Padmanabha Literally 'lotus from the navel' referring to Vishnu reclining on the Naga Ananta; a lotus springs from his navel and Brahma appears from its flower.

Padmapani The one who holds the lotus.

Pala Indian art sytle from the eastern Indian dynasty of the same name.

Parvati Goddess and consort of Shiva.

Phnom Khmer for hill or mountain.

Pradakshina Clockwise and customary procesion around a temple in which the shrine is kept to the right. See also prasavaya.

Prajñaparamita Female form of the Bhodisattva Lokesvara.

Prasavya Anti-clockwise procession around a temple keeping the shrine to the left. Such a direction taken when it is a tomb. See also pradakshina.

Pratibimba Hindu concept of making an earthly representation of a heavenly form.

Preah The Khmer word for sacred.

Puranas The sacred Hindu texts, including the Ramayana and Mahabharata.

Purusa Male person.

Rahu Demon whoe body was cut by Vishnu's discus; responsible for eclipses by his attempts to eat the sun and the moon.

Rama One of the earthly incarnations of Vishnu and eponymous hero of the Ramayana.

Ramakien See Ramayana.

Ramayana Major Hindu romantic epic tracing the efforts and adventures of Rama to recover his wife Sita, who was kidnapped by the demon Ravana. The Thai version is the Ramakien.

Ravana Multi-armed and -headed demon, the villain of the piece in the Ramayana epic.

Rig Veda The earliest Vedic sacred text, meaning 'Wisdom of the Verses', written about 1,400 BC. Its principal myth is the struggle between the major Vedic god Indra and the dragon Vritra.

Rishi Hindu seer, ascetic or sage. Forerunners of the brahmins.

Saivite Pertaining to Shiva.

Sakti The creative force in its feminine form.

Samadhi The deepest form of yoga meditation, in which the ultimate vision is achieved.

Samanakha Thai name for Surpanakha.

Sampot Traditional Khmer garment.

Samsara The endless cycle of life and rebirth.

Sankha Community of Buddhist monks.

Sanskrit Ancient Indian language and script.

Sapta Matrikas 'Seven Divine Mothers' comprising Brahmi, Maheswari, Vaishnavi, Kaumari, Indrani, Varahi and Chamundi.

Satayu Mythical bird, friend of Rama.

Sema Buddhist boundary stone.

Senapati Minister of state.

Sesha See Ananta.

Shiva One of the Hindu Trinity of gods; the God of Destruction, but also of rebirth. Called Isuan in Thai.

Simha Lion.

Simhamukha Literally 'lion face'. Similar to a kala face but with a lower jaw.

Singha See simha.

Sita Wife of Rama.

Soma The drink of Indra, related to the fermented juice of a climbing plant, and to the moon. See somasutra.

Somasutra Conduit for lustral water in the form of a gargoyle, facing north.

Sri Alternative name for Lakshmi; its general meaning is 'auspicious'.

Stele Upright slab bearing inscriptions.

Surgriva Monkey-king ally of Rama in the Ramayana.

Surpanakha Ravana's sister.

Surya The god of the sun, and one of the three principal gods in the Rig Veda (with Indra and Agni).

Sutra Narrative scripture.

Svayambhuvanartha Naturally occuring linga.

Tandava One of Siva's dances in which he brings the universe to destruction and a new beginning.

Tantric Developed from of Hinduism and Mahayana Buddhism in which magic features strongly.

Theravada The traditional form of Buddhism (see Hinayana).

Toranee The Thai name for Bhumidevi.

Trailokyavijaya Literally 'victory of the three worlds' - name given to one of the major Mahayana Bodhisattvas.

Trijata Wife of Ravana's brother, Vibesha.

Trimurti The Hindu trinity of gods: Brahma the Creator, Vishnu the Preserver and Shiva the Destroyer.

Ucchaisaravas Magical horse that emerges from the Churning of the Sea of Milk; later appropriated by Indra.

Uma Shiva's consort.

Umamahesvara Term describing the image of Shiva and his consort, Uma, together.

Ushnisha Protruberance on the head of Buddha, symbolising his all-encompassing knowledge.

Vahana Mount or vehicle of a god. For example, Shiva rides the bull Nandin.

Vaishnavi One of the Sapta Matrikas, or Seven Divine Mothers.

Vaisnavite Pertaining to Vishnu.

Vajra Diamond, thunderbolt.

Vajradhara Literally 'bearer of lightening'; name given to one of the Mahayan Buddhas and also to one of the Mahayana Bodhisattvas.

Vajrasattva One of the six 'meditation Buddhas'.

Vamana or Vamana-avatara The avatar, or incarnation, of Vishnu as dwarf.

Vara-mudra Gesture signifying benediction, in which the right hand is extended palm outwards.

Varaha or varaha-avatara The avatar, or incarnation, of Vishnu as a boar.

Varman, - varman Literally 'chest-armour' and by extension 'protégé'.

Varuna Originally a universal deity,

encompassing the sky, later to become a god of seas and rivers, riding the makara. The guardian of the West.

Vasudeva Father of Krishna.

Vasuki Name of the giant nage used by the gods and demons to churn the Sea of Milk.

Vayu God of air and wind, linked with Indra.

Vedas The four religious books that instruct Brahmanic ritual, the most famous being the Rig Veda composed in the first millenium BC.

Vibeksha Ravana's brother.

Viraba Demon enslaved by Rama.

Viradha One of the giants from the Ramayana.

Vishnu Member of the Hindu Trinity; the Preserver and Protector. The Thai name is Narai. A popular deity among worshippers, he manifests himself on earth in a variety of incarnations, or avatars.

Vishrakarma The divine architectet.

Vitarka-mudra Gesture of preaching and giving a sermon, performed by joining thumb and forefinger, palm held outwards with one hand or both.

Yaksha General term for demon.
Yakshi, yakhsini Female demon.

Yama God of Death and guardian of the South. Son of Surya. His mount is a water buffalo.

Yogini Mahayanic goddess associated with Vajrasattva.

Yuga One of the four ages in the world cycle according to Hinduism. The four ages, and shorter intervening periods of twilight, last 4,320,000 human years, and this is called a mahayuga. 2,000 mahayugas comprise a kalpa.

ARCHITECTURAL TERMS

Acroter Pinnacle or other ornament that stands on a parapet.

Anastylosis Integral restoration in which all the elements of a structure are analysed and numbered; following which the building is made structurally sound and rebuilt with the original stones. Additional materials are only used where structurally necessary.

Antarala Corridor connecting the garbhagra to the mandapa.

Arcature Niche

Ardhamandapa Shallow porch on a mandapa.

Arogayasala Hospital, or more accurately the laterite chapel that was part of a hospital. Like the dharmasala (see below), these were all built during the reign of Jayavaraman VII.

Asrama Monastery.

Baluster Circular-sectioned post or pillar, as in a barred window or the uprights of a balustrade.

Balustrade Railing or similar in which balusters are the uprights surmounted by a beam or coping.

Baray Artificial lake or reservoir.

Colonette Small column, usually decorative in Khmer architecture, standing at either side of a doorway.

Corbel Deeply embedded load-bearing stone projecting from a wall.

Corbel arch False arch built from corbels projecting from opposite walls in tiers so that the topmost stones meet in the centre.

Cornice Decorated projection that corwns or portects an architectural feature such as a doorway. The cornice level is that immediately above the lintels.

Decorative lintel Rectangular stone slab carrying a carved design with important iconographical features; attached above any doorway in a Khmer temple but not having a structurally supportive function.

Dharmasala Commonly used but inaccurate term for the laterite chapels of resting places bult for travellers along the main Khmer highways. These were all built during the reign of Jayavarman VII.

Fronton See pediment.

Functional lintel See structural lintel.

Garbhagrha The inner chamber in a Khmer sanctuary, in the form of a square cell. Literally 'womb house'.

Gopura Entrance pavilion sometime surmounted by a tower.

Laterite Red, porous, iron-bearing rock; easy to quarry and clay-like when wet, but extremely hard when dried.

Library Isolated annexes usually found in pairs on either side and in front of the main sanctuary tower facing west, or at the entrance to an enclosure. This is a traditional name for them although there is no certainty that they were actually used as libraries.

Lintel Stone block spanning an entrance acorss two door pillars. May be load-bearng or purely decorative. See also decorative lintel and structual lintel.

Mandapa Antechamber - a pavilion or porch in front of the main sanctuary.

Pancha Yatana In Hindu religious architecture, a temple with a main central sanctuary surrounded by four other shrines and connected to them by cloisters.

Pediment The triangular vertical feature above the lintel, over a portico or other entrance. Used decoratively and carved with various scenes.

Pilaster Square or rectangular-sectioned pillar that is actually attached to the wall and is thus a projection rather than a free-standing column.

Portico Entrance porch.

Prali Roof finial.

Prang Elongated cone-shaped tower. The central prang is built over the garbhagrha.

Prasat From the Indian 'prasada', a terraced pyramid temple typical of southern India.

Quincunx An arrangement of five objects in which one is placed centrally and the other four occupy the corners. See Pancha Yatana.

Redented Architectural treatment of a structure in plan whereby the corners are indented into successive right-angles.

Sala Rest hall.

Sema Buddhist boundary stone. Its exact funtion in Khmer temples is uncertain, although in Thailand since the 14th century it has been used to delineate Ordination Halls.

Sikhara Pointed tower in Indian architecture.

Somasutra Stone pipe or channel through which the lustral waters used to wash the image inside the sanctuary are drained, projecting outside the temple. Often terminates with a carved makara head at the spout. Indicative of a Saivite temple.

Stele Upright slab bearing inscriptions.

Structural lintel The load-bearing upper part of a stone door frame. Normally largely concealed by the decorative lintel carved with iconographical details.

Stucco Plaster used for covering walls (brick walls in Khmer architecture) or for decorative purposes.

Trimukha Literally 'three-faced'. Three-lobed design of a platform or structure seen in plan.

Vantail Leaf of a door.

Vault Arch extended in depth.

Vihara Rectangular building usually built to house a Buddha image. Viharn in Thai.

Vihear Khmer name for 'viharn'.

Wat General term used for Buddhist temple.

BIBLIOGRAPHY

Anuvit Charernsupkul.
The Structure Types and Pattern Bonds of Khmer and Srivijayan Brick Architecture in Thailand. *Bangkok; 1982.*

Boisselier, J.
Le Cambodge. *Paris: Picard; 1966.*

Boisselier, J.
Trends in Khmer Art.
Ithaca, NY: SEAP; 1989.

Boisselier, J.
Trends in Khmer Art. Cornell:
SEAP; 1989.

Briggs, L.P.
The Ancient Khmer Empire. *Philadelphia: The American Phi1osophical Society; 1951.*

Brown, R.
The Ceramics of South-East Asia (2nd edition).
Singapore: Oxford University Press; 1988.

Chandler, David.
A History of Cambodia. Colorado: Westview Press; 1983.

Childress, Vance.
Final Report of Reconstruction and Excavation of Prasat Ban Pluang. District Prasat. Surin Province. *Thailand. Oklahoma: Soday Research Foundation; 1975.*

Clarac, A. and M. Smithies.
Guide to Thailand. *Bangkok: DK; 1981.*

Dagens, B.
Autour de l'iconographie de Pimay.
Franco-Thai symposium; 1988.

Diskul, M. C. Subhadradis.
Two Khmer Temples: Prasat Phanom Rung and Prasat Muang Singh. The Artistic Heritage of Thailand (National Museum Volunteers. Bangkok. Sawaddi magazine); *1979; 79-88.*

Diskul, M. C. Subhadradis.
Notes on recent excavations at Muang Singh.
JSS, vol 66/1: 1978.

Fine Arts Department.
Prasat Muang Singh. *Bangkok: FAD; 1987.*

Fine Arts Department.
Report of the Survey and Excavations of Ancient Monuments in North-eastern Thailand: Part 2: 1960-61. *Bangkok: FAD; 1961.*

Fine Arts Department.
The Survey and Excavations of Ancient Monuments in North-eastern Thailand.
Bangkok: Fine Arts Dept.; 1959.

Frankel, B.
The Waters. The King and the Mountain: Khmer Cosmology. The Artistic Heritage of Thailand (ed. National Museum Volunteers. Bangkok. Sawaddi Magazine); *1979:67-79.*

Freeman, M. and R. Warner.
Angkor. The Hidden Glories. *1990.*

Hammond, S.
Prasat Phnom Rung: A Khmer temple in Thailand. Arts of Asia; *1988; 18(4): 51-67.*

Jacob, J.
The Ecology of Angkor: Evidence from the Khmer Inscriptions. Nature and Man in South East Asia (ed. P. Stott);
1978; SOAS (London): pp. 109-128.

Jacque, C. Angkor. *1990.*

Manit Vallibhotama.
Guide to Phimai. Bangkok: *FAD; 2504.*

Mazzeo, D. and C. S. Antonini.
Ancient Cambodia. London: Cassell; *1978.*

Moore, E.
Origins of Khmer Naga Legends. Sawaddi;
1981; May-June: 23-28.

Moore, E.
Water Management in Early Cambodia: Evidence from aerial photography. Geographical Journal;
1989; 155(2): 204-214.

National Museum Volunteers Group.
Treasures from the National Museum, Bangkok. *Bangkok: TWP; 1987.*

Penpane Damrongsiri.
The Divine World. Emblems and Motifs. Bangkok: *National Museum; 1988.*

Piriya Krairiksh.
Art Styles in Thailand. Bangkok: *Fine Arts Department; 1977.*

Piriya Krairiksh.
Khmer Ruins in Thailand. Orientations;
1981;12(12):22-33.

Smitthi Siribhradra and Mayuree Veraprasert.
Lintels. A comparative study of Khmer lintels in Thailand and Cambodia.
Bangkok: Siam Commercial Bank; 1989.

Srisakra Vallibhotama.
Prasat Khao Phnom Rung.
Bangkok: Silpawatannatham; 1987.

Stott, Philip.
Angkor: Shifting the hydraulic paradigm. SOAS monograph; *1990.*

Suksvasti. M.R. Suriyavudh
Stone Lintels in Thailand.
Bangkok: Muang Boran; 1988.

Wolters, O. W.
History. Culture and Region in Southeast Asian Perspectives. *Singapore: Institute of South East Asian Studies; 1982.*

Zimmer, Henrich.
Myths and Symbols in Indian Art and Civilization. *Princeton: Bollingen; 1974.*

INDEX

Architectural and Iconographical

Biographical Index

General index

Geographical index

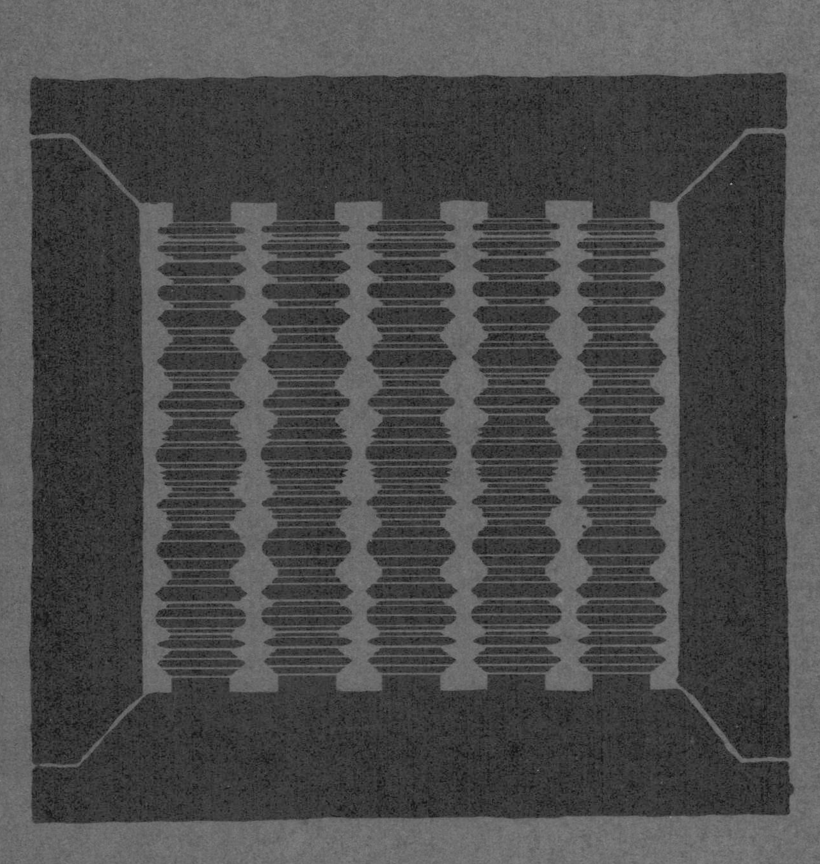